How to Make Money in ISAs and SIPPs

How to Make Money in ISAs and SIPPs

Tax-Efficient Investing Made Easy

STEPHEN SUTHERLAND

Matador
9 Priory Business Park
Kibworth Beauchamp
Leicestershire LE8 0RX, UK
Tel: (+44) 116 279 2299
Fax: (+44) 116 279 2277
Email: books@troubador.co.uk
Web: www.troubador.co.uk/matador

ISBN SB: 978-1783063-284
HB: 978-1783063-291

British Library Cataloguing in Publication Data.
A catalogue record for this book is available from the British Library.

Typeset in 12pt Times New Roman by Troubador Publishing Ltd, Leicester, UK

Matador is an imprint of Troubador Publishing Ltd

This book is dedicated to my parents, Brian and Marie Sutherland, the greatest mum and dad a son could wish for. I love you both so much and greatly appreciate all the help and support you've given to me. You are both amazing!

The Christie
Charitable Fund

How to Make Money in ISAs and SIPPs was compiled in aid of The Christie; a specialised cancer centre. 100% of the book royalties will be donated to the charity. The Christie played a big part in helping our mum fight and beat lung cancer. For their love, help and support, we are truly grateful.

About The Christie

The Christie (Registered Charity Number 1049751) is a specialised cancer centre with a long standing reputation (since 1901) for high quality diagnosis, treatment and care for cancer patients. Based in Manchester and covering a population of 3.2 million, we register around 12,500 new patients and treat about 40,000 patients every year. Approximately 15% of patients, often with complex or rare cancers are referred here from other hospitals around the UK.

Not only is The Christie the largest single-site cancer hospital in Europe, it is also a world-leader in cancer research, from where groundbreaking research has led to the development of many new cancer treatments. Manchester was recently ranked as best in the UK for cancer research. The Christie charity raises funds for patient welfare, cancer research, new buildings and medical equipment. In recent years it has contributed to the new £35 million Patient treatment Centre – housing our comprehensive Chemotherapy Unit and the world's largest Clinical trials Phase I Unit, together with a £7 million Critical Care Unit – enabling us to perform rare and complex surgery and subsequent isolation. Also we have, in the last

2 years, opened 2 satellite Radiotherapy Units at Oldham Royal and Salford Royal hospitals.

In addition, the charity pays for all the extra special services, such as complementary therapies, the wig service, benefits advice and counselling, that help to make living with cancer a little easier. Thank you all again for your wonderful support, without which The Christie would not be the place it is today, our patients wouldn't be living longer and being diagnosed and treated earlier with the most state – of-the-art equipment and medicines.

Praise for *How to Make Money in ISAs and SIPPs*

As well as asking respected journalists, authors and thought leaders to review my book, I also asked a selection of my clients. Below are just a few of them to whet your appetite, however in 'Appendix 5: Book Reviews', you can find them all. Enjoy!

"With his newest book, Stephen Sutherland is ready to spread the wealth! Having realized the power of the stock market in his own portfolio as well as his clients', Sutherland takes the time to reveal some of his 'secrets' for choosing the market's best funds.

I found this book incredibly easy to read and understand. Sutherland spends time on the concepts that matter. For anyone looking to take a more active role in their investing, *How to Make Money in ISAs and SIPPs* is a great resource . . . and an easy read. It walks you through the benefits of the UK's two tax-efficient accounts before revealing some actionable strategies you can use to unlock the power of the market.

Your brain is often the enemy of your returns, and I'm glad Sutherland spent time identifying some of the behavioral shortcomings investors face. Make no mistake: Buy-and-hold investing is not dead! Even though Sutherland's approach is more technical than what we preach at The Motley Fool, he values consistency, performance, and tenure in management teams . . . and we Fools can't argue with that!"

Jill Ralph, Managing Director, The Motley Fool UK

"Stephen, thanks for producing such an excellent book. You should be rightly proud of it. It was a pleasure to read it (three times). *How to Make Money in ISAs and SIPPs* is a MUST READ for anyone who invests money in funds. The book takes you from the basics of understanding the ISA and SIPP wrapper, through to the all important aspect of how to pick good funds and manage your portfolio. It is written in an easy to follow, logical order which covers the subject in a very comprehensive way, catering for anyone less familiar with the subject, right through to the more seasoned investor.

The process of picking good funds is covered in detail in Chapter 6 and the information in this chapter alone is worth the price of the book. There are many graphical examples included in the book, which aids the understanding of the concepts discussed, including step by step screen shots detailing how to check a fund's performance and characteristics. I was delighted to see that Stephen also covered the psychology of investing within Chapter 9. In my opinion, as a more seasoned investor, this is one of the critical aspects that an investor must understand if they are going to be successful in the markets.

Stephen's enthusiasm for the markets and the depth of his knowledge on the subject are clear throughout the book. His positive attitude to life shines through right from the outset and this combination of knowledge and enthusiasm has produced a book which is easy to read and understand, whether you are a seasoned participant in the market or completely new to the subject. I'd go as far as to say turning to the next page is compelling. That's not something that can be said for many books on finance. I also think this book should be compulsory reading for all senior secondary school children as they set out into the world. I certainly wish it had been around when I was at that stage.

The book should at the very least, be on everybody's investment book shelf but it would serve you better being on your desk. It's an excellent book which I will be referring to over and over again. 5 stars."

Ray Hughes, ISACO Client, Entrepreneur and Private Investor

"A thorough and very useful guide to investing in ISAs and SIPPs, and well timed. There are now a huge number of 'orphan investors' without an IFA as a direct result of RDR, and the information provided in this book gives them much needed support. Easy to read and follow, and put into context throughout. The information on charges is particularly useful."

Josh Ausden, Editor, FE Trustnet

"Dear Stephen, firstly I would like to complain as I could not stop reading your new book! My plan was to have a quick look at it then read it on a long flight later this week! I will need to buy another book now! Seriously though, I think your book is excellent. I found it's written in a simple way to understand so that non-financial professional people like me can grasp the points.

I have lots of books about investing and mostly they are complicated and to be honest, boring. I enjoyed reading your new book and could not put it down – it just makes so much sense. I guess the part of the book I most enjoyed was 'Chapter 9: Beyond Greed and Fear' – I found myself saying 'that's me' and I can fully recognise this behavioural finance, which is a very interesting subject. I would rate the book with 5 stars.

It's now been four years since I became a client of yours, I fully believe in your concept and have made good returns, it's a great system. I also love the fact that you have very kindly donated your royalties from the new book to the Christie Charity. Very well done to you and your team and keep up the good work."

David Mountain, ISACO Client and Engineer

"At last a common-sense, easy to understand book that proves you don't need to have an MBA or be a financial whizz kid to build a healthy retirement pot. And you can do it all using legitimate tax breaks in the form of SIPPs and ISAs that the government and HMRC fully approve of. Stephen estimates he has spent over 20,000 hours perfecting his investment technique, but his book allows you to learn many of his simple skills in the space of a few hours.

This book is a worthwhile read for the new or fairly experienced private investor – and maybe even a few so-called professional investors. You don't have to want or believe you can be a millionaire from reading it, but it will help you take control of your own savings and make better investment decisions. This book could be the best investment you've ever made."

Lawrence Gosling, Founding Editor of Investment Week

"One day I realised that to secure my future, I would have to learn more about investing some of my hard-earned money. I read several books and courses but found it difficult to glean much. I didn't learn much from a few financial investment advisors I met and considerably less from some bank advisors.

As for most of the graphs they produced whilst advising me, I was more confused than ever.

Then along came Stephen Sutherland and his company ISACO with his book *Liquid Millionaire* and then his new book 'How to Make Money in ISAs and SIPPs' with the sub-title, 'Tax-Efficient Investment Made Easy'.

Stephen's books were a breath of fresh air to me – full of knowledge, detail and his expertise, in fact a work of art in explaining how to improve your returns on every pound you invest and also how you can avoid some of the high and hidden charges that can reduce your returns.

A huge bonus is how Stephen writes in such an easily understood and interesting style.

The documented proof of his record in helping others to improve their investments made me realise I had found the mentor I needed to help secure my financial goals. Stephen's book allows you to be a 'fly on the wall – look over his shoulder' at exactly how he selects his investments.

My advice to you is to read the book (I give it a 5 star rating) – then take action on Stephen's advice. You might also decide to become a personal client as I did, which allows me to simply follow the decisions he makes, it's so easy. Another really great thing I like, is that he keeps all his clients informed of everything he is doing investment-wise every single day, which takes just 3 to 4 minutes to read. If you do read the book it could change your life and your financial success – as it has mine and continues to do so."

Bob Sweeney, ISACO Client and Private Investor

"What a wonderful book. The arguments regarding investing via ISAs and SIPPs are well argued and fascinating."

Alan Miller, SCM Private Chief Investment Officer

"I became a client of Stephen's after reading his first book *Liquid Millionaire* in 2010. I read a lot of the financial press and get confused by most of it. Stephen's very clear and straightforward approach seemed to me to have real integrity. I have not regretted my decision. I just wish I had found Stephen, and his brother Paul, ten years earlier!!

Practice makes perfect, and *How to Make Money in ISAs and SIPPs* is an even better and clearer read than Stephen's first book. His style is engagingly free of jargon, and is very easy to read. The book is very well structured. He explains what ISAs and SIPPs are and why they are so important. Importantly, he goes into the all too often grey area of fees and how to minimise them. But most importantly, he clearly explains the critical importance of when to invest in which funds AND when to exit from them.

There is no doubt this book will greatly help a novice investor, and even experienced ones, to pick funds and time them accurately. Personally I leave all of that to Stephen and Paul, and so far their track record is very impressive indeed. But whether you let them take the strain or do it yourself, read this book – it can only help. I would unequivocally give it a 5 star rating!!"

John W. Cornwell, ISACO Client and Consultant Chartered Town Planner

"A very readable book dispelling a lot of myths that stand between investors and financial security. This book is particularly suitable for beginners, the people who know little about investing but who stand to gain most. It is set out logically so that you progress seamlessly from one topic to the next, learning all the way."

Rodney Hobson, Bestselling Author, *Shares Made Simple, The Dividend Investor, How to Build a Share Portfolio, Understanding Company News and Small Companies, Big Profits*

"I wish that I had read this book 20 years ago. It would have radically changed my saving and investing strategies and would have dramatically improved my financial position today. Stephen Sutherland's book *How to Make Money in ISAs and SIPPs* has opened my eyes to the major benefits of investing in ISAs and SIPPs, and in his sections on myths, dispelled a number of erroneous ideas I had.

I particularly liked his informal writing style; it is almost like having a friend by your side giving you their advice. The book is packed with useful information and guides the reader on how to choose suitable funds to invest and how to minimise their charges and costs. My favourite chapters were *Beyond Greed and Fear* because most of the content was new to me; *How to Manage Your Portfolio* because it identifies resources that I never knew existed and *Creating an Income for Life* because it has provoked me into thinking about my timescales for investment.

I also liked the fact that Stephen describes his results in both his good and bad years and how his investment approach has significantly developed and improved over the period that he has studied ISAs and SIPPs. This book is a must buy for anyone who is serious about building up wealth for their retirement, or for helping their children invest for their future. 5 stars!"

Jeff Hall, ISACO Client and Business Owner

"I'm not sure what's controversial about this. Make as much money as you can in the market, and pay as little of it as possible to the tax man. If you blow the last part, you might as well have blown the first part. So, wrap your high-performing portfolio in tax protection with the ideas in this book."

Jason Kelly, Bestselling Author of *The Neatest Little Guide to Stock Market Investing*

"I found this book extremely informative for investors, particularly those investing in ISAs and SIPPs, and for others who are trying to optimize their investment returns. It explains simply and in sufficient detail for the less knowledgeable how to take advantage of these tax-efficient schemes, how to ensure you're invested in the best funds and manage your portfolio effectively and how to determine whether we're heading for a bull or bear market i.e. when to get in, stay in or get out. It also suggests how to create regular income from your investments but is not for those wanting to earn a quick buck; it takes a long term view.

Before becoming an ISACO client I read Stephen's previous book *Liquid Millionaire,* which led me to believe that 'shadow investing' for our ISAs was the way to go. I feel much better informed now, particularly on selecting the best funds, how to read the markets and the different charging rates levied by financial advisors. How to use Morningstar for fund information, Investors.com for what the market is doing and various other references will improve my knowledge and get me more interested in reviewing my investments regularly.

The book has been well researched by the author and follows a logical sequence, making it easy to put down and pick up again or to use as a reference point when looking for investment information. It stresses that portfolios need to be managed on a full time basis, which most private individuals can't do and so they need professional help.

I give the book a 5 star rating and recommend it to all ISACO clients and prospects, anyone who wants to improve the performance of their portfolios and financial advisors."

John Wallace, ISACO Client and Ex-CIO of One of the World's Leading International Banks

"How to Make Money in ISAs and SIPPs by Stephen Sutherland is a book explaining how to do exactly as the title suggests. I agreed to read and review the book as a client of ISACO and I must admit I was not looking forward to it as I always find this sort of book quite boring to read.

I am an avid investor, always have been, but I do find reading about the subject quite dull, which is probably why I have never been any good at it! I actually read this book in just three evenings, I found it very easy to read and I didn't want to put it down. I found the chapter for beginners very informative and easy to understand and this ease of reading carried on throughout the rest of the book. Graphs and illustrations helped to explain things in a very straightforward and unstuffy manner.

I also found the sincerity of the author coming through, at one point apologising for not guiding his clients into a cash park prior to the stock market's plummet in 2008. I would thoroughly recommend this book to investors old, new and those considering becoming clients of ISACO. I award the book full marks, five stars out of five."

Paul Parkin, ISACO Client and Business Owner

For the complete list of reviews, go to Appendix 5: Book Reviews.

Acknowledgements

I'd like to start by saying a huge thank you to my mum, dad and brother Paul – you are three very special people in my life and without your immense help, this book would not have become a reality. Thank you so much for believing in me. My sincere and heartfelt gratitude also goes to all of our clients, especially the ones who kindly agreed to review this book. Thank you, thank you, thank you!

Staying on the subject of book reviews, I'd like to say a big thank you to Lee Clarke and Jeff Hall for helping with the book's structure. I'd also like to say a big 'cheers' to all the journalists, authors and corporate executives who also very kindly agreed to review this book. I want to also thank Siobhan Curham, my extremely talented editor for her brilliant editing and proofing work.

I'd surely like to thank Steve Todd, my friend and ISACO's Global Market Strategist, who created many of the countless images that are featured in this book. I also want to thank George Foster for the amazing book cover design and say a big thank you to Helen McCusker for helping us promote the book. For helping my life run smoothly, I'd like to say thank you to my PA, Karen Harrop and housekeeper, Teresa O'Mara. My thanks also go to ISACO's financial director Paul Cooper and ISACO's business administrator Chris Elmes.

Tim, Ileen, Sue and Jason from Easiprint, you've also been a huge help – thanks! I'd also like to say a big thank you to Steve Oakman from Concentric Marketing, Jeremy Thompson, Jennifer Liptrot, Rachel Gregory, Terry Compton, Sarah Taylor and Rosie Grindrod from Troubador Publishing, Angie at MarketSmith for helping me to obtain image and content permissions, and to Jon Sands for making sure all my facts were correct regarding ISAs and SIPPs.

My gratitude also extends to two companies that we like to think of as partners of ours – Fidelity and Morningstar. I'd also like to say thanks to all my mentors, who include William O'Neil, Brian Tracy and Sir Richard Branson, plus the countless authors I've read and seminar leaders I've seen and listened to. I'd like to close with thanking you, the reader – deciding to take time out to read this book means the world to me and I do hope that one day we meet up. You never know, in the future we may even become friends.

Contents

Foreword

You may well be scratching your head and asking yourself, 'who is Richard Koch?' Allow me to briefly present my credentials, before saying why I think this book and its author should be taken very seriously.

At the age of 40, I 'retired' from a career in business. I'd been a specialist in business strategy, as a consultant with the Boston Consulting Group, a partner of Bain & Company, and co-founder of L.E.K. Consulting. I decided to stop working ridiculous hours, get a life, and in my spare time pursue two hobbies I enjoyed – writing books, and investing.

I've been fortunate with both. I'm in the *Sunday Times* Rich List – they say I have net assets after tax of around £140m, which apparently makes me joint number 572 on the UK list, behind Mick Jagger (£200m) but ahead of David Bowie (£100m), who deserves the money far more than me – and may well need it much more too!

I began with nothing, and nearly all my money has been made from investment, not starting seriously until 1990. Matthew Goodman of *The Sunday Times* of May 5th 2013 said that I "am regarded as a savvy and meticulous investor". I'm the author of *The 80/20 Principle* which has sold more than a million copies worldwide, and also of *The Financial Times Guide to Selecting Shares That Perform*

– which is now in its fourth edition and has nice reviews[1]. If you'd like to learn more about me and my views, eccentric or otherwise, please follow me on Twitter or visit www.richardkoch.net – I write a weekly blog which appears on Monday afternoons.[2]

How did I come to be writing this Foreword?

I first came across Stephen Sutherland at the end of 2008 when I reviewed his first book, *Liquid Millionaire*. I liked the book, but was taken aback by his unapologetically bullish views – he said the stock market was about to soar at a time when it seemed the world was coming to an end. I thought he was crazy to be so definite that the market was about to go up.

Well, to my surprise, he was right. Since then I have kept in close touch and I receive his *Daily Market Updates*, which have proved instructive and profitable for me. Reading the Update is a key part of my daily routine and one of the few emails I read extremely carefully, word for word. The same is true of his wonderfully insightful monthly summary, *The Big Picture*, which has great graphs that even I can understand.

I have discovered that Stephen is a warm, sincere, and likeable person, someone I would willingly follow into dark and unlikely places. The guy is smart, decent, and honest – but that is not a good enough reason to follow him. Here are six reasons why I do:

- His track record is excellent.
- He knows how to find and invest in funds likely to beat the market.

- He will help you time your market entry and exit. Timing is everything. Nobody can guarantee you accuracy on this. But Stephen gives you clues and guidance that is second to none, and he does it in a fun way.
- He will help you understand the daily psychology of the market, so you can get into sync with professional investors. It's well known that most individual investors under-perform the professionals. To stand a chance in competing against them, you need some astute advice so you can trade with the trend instead of against it. Momentum is terribly important, and few private investors respect it enough.
- He will help you keep all trading costs and charges really low. I hate transactions costs. Over the long haul, they make a big difference. Stephen hates these costs too and will show you how to minimize them.
- Finally, I think he's an expert in ISA and SIPP investments, which are the most tax-efficient devices available to most UK investors, especially those on high incomes.

And that, ladies and gentlemen, is all I think I need to say. Enjoy the book that follows, but most important, take appropriate action afterwards. Investment should be enjoyable as well as enriching. Thank you for reading this, and I hope you will take a peek at my website and blogs!

Richard Koch
Gibraltar, June 2013

Introduction

Do you desire an income for life? Are you looking for a simple way to boost your investment returns? Is your aim a secure and richer retirement? If you answered yes to any of these questions, then this book is for you.

In the coming chapters, I'm going to show you how Individual Savings Accounts (ISAs) and Self Invested Personal Pensions (SIPPs) – two extremely tax-efficient 'wrappers' – can help you to beat the market, increase your returns and create an income for life. I'm going to share with you how to find best of breed investments and tell you when to buy and when to sell.

I'll also give you insider secrets for keeping your trading costs low and show you the biggest mistakes DIY (Do It Yourself) investors make and the best ways to avoid them. If you class yourself as a DIY investor who is looking for better returns and financial security in your retirement, you are going to love this book.

How to Make Money in ISAs and SIPPs started as a series of articles on our investment blog, so a lot of the content you are about to read has been taken from many of the popular reports and guides I have written over the last 18 months. *How to Make Money in ISAs and SIPPs* is an expansion, organisation and simplification of that work. If you have downloaded and read some of my material in the past, thank you so much – it really does mean the world to me.

Two of the UK's best-kept investment secrets

ISAs and SIPPs are two of the UK's best-kept investment secrets. They are known as 'wrappers' and are great, tax-efficient shelters to help you build and preserve tax-free wealth. All adults with savings or investments should have an ISA or SIPP, otherwise they are simply handing money to the taxman needlessly. ISAs have been extremely successful. According to figures from HM Revenue & Customs, in 2011, £200.6 billion was invested in cash ISAs and £190.3 billion was invested in stocks and shares ISAs and PEPs.

During the tax year of 2011–12, one in every four people in the UK bought an ISA[3] and one in every thirty of us subscribed to a stocks and shares ISA[4]. But what about pensions? Have they been as popular as ISAs? The statistics tell us that an impressive £19.1 billion was contributed to personal pensions in 2010–11[5], one in every seven of us has a personal pension[6] and almost one in every sixty of us has a SIPP[7].

Why I wrote this book

It's sad but true that the average investor underperforms the market by a wide margin[8]. But it's not just private investors who underperform – most financial professionals also fail to beat the indexes[9]. This happens for a number of reasons but if you pressed me for a short answer, I'd say that this is due to a lack of knowledge.

When some people hear about underperformance, their response is, *so what*? However, when they learn that for private investors, underperforming the market has serious consequences and potentially devastating effects later on in life, they sit up straight in their chairs. You see, when you underperform, it not only means you are likely to fail to reach your financial goals, it also means you could run out of cash during your later years – a fear that for most people is worse than death[10].

That's why I wrote this book. It was to share with you the key information you may be missing in order to achieve better returns on your investment portfolio. My aim is that the information I pass on to you – when put into action – will increase the probability of you outperforming the market over the coming years.

If you do beat the market it will play a big part in helping you reach your financial objectives on time. Reaching those objectives may also help you create enough capital to enable you to enjoy a comfortable, stress-free retirement and benefit from never having to worry about money again. Now, that would be nice, wouldn't it?

Where I can help

In the years following the financial crisis, we noticed that individual investors who were angry with the stock market and disappointed by the performance of their so-called expert advisers have been taking it upon themselves to make their own investment decisions.

We noticed that once they made sure that their money was out of the hands of the professionals and the obligation to direct their investments was squarely on their own shoulders, many weren't quite sure where to begin. Fuelled by anxiety about where to put their money, they found themselves asking questions like: *What do I do now? When do I buy? When do I sell?*

This is where I can help and hopefully ease the anxiety. My expertise lies in four areas:

1) How to find and invest in funds likely to beat the market
2) How to time your buys and exits with greater accuracy
3) How to get in sync with the market and trade with the trend instead of against it
4) How to keep all associated costs, charges and fees low

My hope is that you'll be interested in brushing up on your skills in one or more of these areas and you'll find benefit in what I have to share.

Who this book is aimed at

How to Make Money in ISAs and SIPPs is aimed at ISA and SIPP investors – or those thinking of investing in ISAs or SIPPs – who are unhappy with their investment performance and want to boost their returns. It's for UK residents either approaching retirement or in retirement.

It's perfect for business owners, self-employed professionals, corporate executives, wealthy retirees and financial professionals such as independent financial advisers (IFAs), wealth managers and pension trustees. It's ideal for individuals who class themselves as either DIY investors, sophisticated investors or financial professionals. It's also essential reading for investors who have at least £250,000 actively invested.

The essence of this book

The best way to explain the essence of this book's message is to use a simple formula.

Money invested in funds + tax-free wrapper + time = creating a lifetime income

As you can see from the formula, if you invest in funds protected by a tax shelter (such as an ISA or SIPP) over a period of time, the capital you'll build up creates an income for life.

What you'll learn

How to Make Money in ISAs and SIPPs is jam-packed with information that I'm certain you'll find useful. It's loaded to the brim with tips, ideas and strategies that you'll hopefully find to be of tremendous value. Because I have no idea of your current level of skill and experience, my aim is to cater for all types of investors. Some of the prospective clients we speak to have very limited knowledge, while some have an extensive understanding.

Some haven't got a clue what an investment fund is, whereas the more advanced investors we talk to are well versed in the basics but lack understanding with things such as effective fund selection, timing their buys and exits, gauging market direction and knowing how to professionally manage their portfolio.

Whether you are new to the game or see yourself as a more seasoned, sophisticated investor, I'm certain that you will find something of benefit in reading this book.

In **Chapter 1: My Story**, you'll learn that I'm Manchester born and completely self-taught. You'll discover that I didn't attend a private school, don't talk with a plum in my mouth, nor do I have some fancy MBA from the London Business School. You'll learn that I'm just your regular, average guy who has a serious love for investing in the stock market.

Just like you, I'm a DIY investor. In this first chapter you'll also discover how I found my true passion in life at age 30, and how my brother and I made £107,543 in one day. We used half of it to buy our dad a Bentley Continental.

In **Chapter 2: ISAs – Aiming to become an ISA Millionaire**, you'll find everything you need to know about this beautifully constructed tax-efficient shelter. I'm sure you'll be excited when you learn how it's possible to become an ISA millionaire through the power of compound interest. I'm also going to share with you a very useful ISA FAQ and dispel 13 ISA myths. Whether you are new to ISAs or whether you consider yourself an expert, I'm certain that you'll enjoy this fact-filled chapter.

In **Chapter 3: SIPPs – the Smarter Way to Manage Your Pension**, I'll show you why SIPPs are a fantastic vehicle for building and preserving tax-free wealth. In this chapter, I'm also going to show you how SIPPs give you full control of your pension, provide generous tax benefits and offer flexible options for taking an income in retirement.

In **Chapter 4: Charges, Fees and Fund Supermarkets**, we'll look at how fund supermarkets can provide you with an excellent way to buy and manage funds at low cost. We'll also look at the different types of supermarkets and I'll give you top tips on what to look for when selecting one. We'll then delve deep into the total cost of fund investing, plus we'll discuss the underhand tactics employed by the investment industry and how to avoid them.

In **Chapter 5: A Quick Guide to Investment Funds**, you'll learn all you need to know about funds in an easy, time condensed way. You'll discover what a fund is, the numerous benefits of fund investing, the risks, types of funds and the key differences between managed funds and trackers.

In **Chapter 6: How to Pick a Good Fund**, you are going to learn my unique strategy for choosing funds that perform; funds that are 'in the money flow' and exhibit superior sustainable growth potential.

In this chapter, I'm also going to introduce you to my 7 tips for fund picking success and 'The Performance Quadrant' – a tool I developed to help determine your future expected return. You're also going to discover HIRE CAR™, a fund screening tool I created that provides guidance and help when looking for quality investment funds.

In **Chapter 7: Fund Timing – When to Buy and When to Exit**, you'll discover all you need to know about when to buy a fund, whether to hold and when to exit. You'll find out how to buy a fund at the optimum time and why it's key to recognise two specific trading patterns and how to determine ideal buy points. You'll also discover the three things I use to help me decide when to sell a fund and why I don't always use stop losses.

In **Chapter 8: Gauging Stock Market Direction**, we'll look at why you need to trade with the trend and not against it. I'll also show you exactly how to analyse the market's health, why you need to keep a close eye on the behaviour of leading stocks and how to protect yourself from market downturns. I'll also give you my take on how to identify market tops, how to spot market bottoms and additional ways to pick up on key market turning points.

In **Chapter 9: Beyond Greed and Fear**, you'll learn about the fascinating subject of behavioural finance and how it can help you make better decisions and improve your investment returns. If, like me, you are fascinated by human behaviour and how most of us behave in odd and irrational ways, you are going to love this chapter.

In **Chapter 10: How to Manage Your Portfolio**, we'll explore the term 'beating the market' and look at the dangers of underperformance. In this chapter, you'll also discover the four questions you need to ask on a daily basis, how to deal with market volatility, strategies for low and medium risk investors, options for entering the market, how to make switches and ways you can add capital.

We'll also look at how you measure investment success, how to cope with temporary losses and a method to help preserve your ISA and SIPP wealth in volatile and falling markets. We'll close this chapter with a comprehensive list of the tools and resources that I personally use, and the good news is that many of them are free.

Chapter 11: Creating an Income for Life is crammed with useful information, but one thing I think you are going to love is my 5 step plan for creating a lifetime income. In this chapter I'm also going to tell you why 'lifestyling' is a flawed and totally outdated strategy.

I'm also going to show you a great strategy I'm currently executing on behalf of my dad, who is looking to invest a significant amount of capital into the market. I'm certain that you'll be lifted when you discover that it's a perfect solution for leaving a legacy and an excellent way to achieve a 7–10% annual return on capital outside your ISA and SIPP.

And finally, in **Chapter 12: A Golden Opportunity**, I'm going to share with you what I believe to be a golden opportunity and how you could potentially profit from it. I'm also going to show you stacked up evidence to suggest that now is probably a very good time to invest. We'll examine the topic of lost decades, why the long term is so important, the resilience of the markets and how the market has historically had periods of strength after periods of weakness. I'd be very surprised if this final chapter doesn't get you excited.

Reading tips for all types of investors

If you class yourself as a beginner when it comes to investing, I suggest you read the book in its entirety. Simply start at Chapter One and move through the rest of the chapters in the order they are written. However, if you are a more seasoned investor who knows all about funds, ISAs, SIPPs and trading platforms, I recommend you read Chapter One (almost everybody likes that chapter) and then jump straight to Chapter Six and continue reading from that point onwards.

By jumping to Chapter Six, as an experienced investor, you can avoid a lot of the things you already know. You'll also get straight to the most valuable part of the book – my personal investment strategy.

Why the US carries a lot of weight

As you read this book, you'll begin to notice a definite and deliberate emphasis on the US stock market. Even though I like to keep an eye on all the world exchanges, my main focus has always been on the US markets and there are four reasons why I do this:

1) The US is the world's largest economy
2) The US is the leading market to watch for clues of future direction
3) The US stock market indexes long-term growth exceeds other world exchanges
4) My philosophy involves watching the behaviour of US institutional investors

As you will soon discover, daily studying of the price and volume action of the US markets helps me get in sync with the market's trend and direction. When some people hear about this deliberate emphasis on the US stock market, they mistakenly think that I only buy US investments. This is not the case.

As you will see in **Chapter 6: How to Pick a Good Fund**, my guideline rules say that the investment fund I buy can invest anywhere in the world. The key, as you will see, is to invest in funds that are being managed by star fund managers – managers who are right in the middle of the money flow.

My aim: plain English and jargon free

I like to keep things simple. I try to avoid long fancy words and stay away from terms that are likely to cause confusion. In my mind, even though the stock market can appear to be complex, how it works and how to invest in it can be simplified into layman's terms. Most of my clients compliment me on my clear communication skills and, throughout this book, I'll talk in plain English and attempt to stay away from any jargon.

If there are any topics that are technical in nature, I'll do my very best to make them easier to understand and throughout the text I'll use a lot of examples, charts and illustrations to make sure that you are with me all the way.

Please feel free to contact me directly with any feedback. My email address is Stephen@ISACO.co.uk.

One of the things that many of my long-term clients know about me is that during my early investing years, I managed to turn a starting amount of $31,409 into $1.28 million over a 38 month period.

Would you like to know how I did it?

Good, because now it's time to share with you…

1. My Story

'An investment in knowledge always pays the best interest.'
– Benjamin Franklin

I was born in 1968 in a small terraced house in Oldham, Lancashire. I was brought up in a very loving, encouraging environment and we were very lucky to have such fantastic parents. I say we were lucky because I have an older sister, Sharon, born in 1966 and a younger brother, Paul, born in 1971. The three of us were all brought up to respect and value money and were never spoilt.

We were raised with a very strong work ethic, which meant that if we wanted something, we had to work for it. From the age of about 12 or 13 I worked part time before school started and at weekends. I was never shy of work and always wanted more money so that I could have the finer things in life. I was a paperboy for a while, as well as a golf caddy. From the age of 14 I worked for Dad almost every school holiday as an apprentice painter and decorator. During my school years – even though I was fairly bright – I hated exams.

It will probably come as no surprise to you then, that I did poorly in the qualification department, leaving at age 16 with just one CSE grade one qualification. In maths I remember getting an 'F'. I said no to college and university and instead went to work for my dad, continuing as an apprentice painter and decorator.

My weekly wage was just under £50. Dad, a self-made man, started out as a painter and decorator and transformed his small business into a successful cleaning and maintenance company that, at its peak, was turning over about £2 million per year. In 1987, when I was 19, Dad started to teach me how his business worked.

This was part of his bigger plan to eventually pass the business on to his children. Over the next 10 years I dug in and learned all that I could about how to manage a business. In 1998, I was primed and ready to take the reins but I knew that if I wanted to take the family business to the next level, I was going to need some help.

The telephone call that changed the direction of my life

Around that time, I remember receiving a telephone call from a marketing company called Results Corporation. A very friendly guy called Chris Billington Hughes told me that they had a proven way to grow small businesses. I remember buzzing from their ideas and I loved their philosophy, which was simply: learn from the experts. Shortly after teaming up with Results, we started receiving monthly newsletters, which included book recommendations.

I had not read a book since school, but these book recommendations had really juicy titles – I just had to take a look at them to find out what they were all about. One of their recommendations was a personal development book written by success guru, Tony Robbins. It was called *Awaken the Giant Within*. I loved it so much that I immediately bought my brother, Paul, a copy. He also read it cover to cover – and loved it just as much as I did.

Success leaves a trail

It was around this point that we both discovered a principle called 'modelling'. Put simply, this is when you copy the strategy of an expert and, if you do it correctly, you get the same result as them. It was also around this time that I awoke to the realisation that in life, there are no action replays. I remember starting to think more clearly about what I wanted from my life, and I soon realised that Dad's cleaning and maintenance business was not what I wanted.

So I started to ask myself questions such as: *What would be your dream job? What work would you love to do even if you weren't paid? What job would give you the greatest feeling of importance?* The answers to these questions all seemed to centre on becoming a full-time stock market professional, which I'd always had a keen interest in, right from an early age.

William O'Neil: a leading stock market authority with 50 years' experience

My plan was simple: to become very good at investing and, in order to do that, I was going to learn from the best. After attending a four day financial seminar in October 1999, one of the speakers, a professional investor, kept referring to someone called Bill O'Neil. I had never heard of Bill O'Neil at the time but, due to the numerous references to him, I knew I would have to look him up after the seminar was over.

I was so pleased when I discovered that Bill O'Neil was a leading authority on the stock market with over 50 years' experience. In fact,

Bill's past results meant that he would be an absolutely perfect person to model. I soon discovered that O'Neil was a living stock market legend whose 50 year method of investing apparently worked in both good times and bad.

Of course, I was a little sceptical at first, but when I delved deeper and learned that with his method, he had not missed the start of a single bull market (up market) in the last 50 years[11], I was sold. What added to my belief were his trading results; I discovered that he made a 2000%+ gain on his portfolio in just 26 months. *Wow*, I thought, *this guy must really know what he's doing.*

Total immersion

I decided to immerse myself totally in O'Neil's philosophy on investing. I read all of O'Neil's books, as well as all of the books O'Neil recommended. I listened intently to all of his audio programmes and eventually subscribed to O'Neil's premium equity research package. I also flew across the Atlantic twice to see him in person.

I first saw him speak in 2001 in South Beach, Miami and again in New York in 2002. After reading O'Neil's bestselling book, *How to Make Money in Stocks*, I started to paper trade the market, which I found to be a good way to learn the ropes without risking any money. As soon as I gained confidence, I set up a trading account with brokerage company Ameritrade, with a starting amount of $31,409 – about £19,000. This was in May 2000.

One of the worst bear markets in the stock market's entire history

Little did I know that I had started my stock investing apprenticeship at a time when the market had just begun what was going to be known as one of the worst bear markets (down markets) in history. Every time I got a confirmation that the trend was up, I started to trade using O'Neil's method as my guide. To ensure that I didn't run out of money, I had to adopt good money management principles.

I used very small amounts of capital and always kept tight 7% stop losses on each and every trade. This meant that if a stock I owned dropped 7% below my buy price, I would sell it immediately. By doing this, I knew that I would have to make literally hundreds of bad trades to lose all of my starting capital. This gave me the confidence to take my time and create good investment habits. The uptrends that I was trading turned out to be bear market rallies, which meant that after a period of between a few weeks and several months, the uptrend became a downtrend.

Beat the market by 40.6%

This meant I was forced out onto the sidelines into the safety of cash. While waiting on the sidelines, I had to patiently sit tight for another confirmation of an uptrend. A valid confirmation came from various indicators, such as how the main indexes were acting and how leading stocks were behaving.

The study and countless hours that I'd invested slowly started to pay off. Unbelievably, during that first year (2000), my account actually saw a gain. Even though I made very little money, I somehow managed to beat the market by 40.6%. This first year's result inspired me to get even more aggressive with my personal development – plus I increased the amount of hours that I was devoting to the market.

I was fortunate to beat the top UK fund manager

In 2001, the second year of what is now known as probably the worst bear market in history, I managed to return 31.74% – beating the NASDAQ Composite, the US technology index, by 52.79%. I was shocked but also proud to learn that my 2001 return beat the top UK fund manager, Ashley Willing, who was managing a fund called *Gartmore UK Focus*.

Incidentally, this was an investment fund that returned 13.72% for the year. This early success of mine spurred me on even further and helped give my confidence as an investor a serious boost. In October 2002 I recognised that the market had found a bottom, but I did not jump in until I was absolutely certain that the great bear market was over.

Could I borrow a million pounds, please?

Because I had learnt that the big money is normally made in the first two years of a new bull market, I decided to contact our bank manager to ask if he would consider lending me £1 million. The bank manager thought I had lost the plot.

'Do you know that the US and Iraq are in conflict and a war could soon erupt?' he said. 'What if Saddam Hussein uses chemical and biological warfare?'

Undeterred, due to my conviction that something big was about to happen, I moved to Plan B, which was to raise cash by equity-releasing money from our home. Because of my absolute certainty in my abilities, we decided to bet the ranch. This was also based on my concrete belief that we had just entered a brand new bull market. The house also belonged to Paul, and so I had to convince him that it would be a sound idea to release close to a quarter of a million pounds from our home. Paul backed me all the way.

The Three Amigos

In May 2003, I took the money from the equity release and wired it to our joint trading account. This amounted to $416,472.90. I was right about my prediction that a new bull market had begun. My decision to raise the money and get it into the market started to pay off. Early on in the bull run, I latched on to three beautiful stocks which we later named 'The Three Amigos'. They were three white-hot Chinese internet stocks with stock ticker symbols SINA, NTES and SOHU.

My method for picking the best stocks was working! These picks of mine probably turned out to be the three biggest winning stocks of the 2003–2007 bull market. SINA made a gain of 4753% in 27 months, SOHU jumped 8246% in 27 months and NTES surged 13746%, again over a 27 month period.

By investing heavily into these stocks and using leverage from Ameritrade and day trading buying power (even more leverage), it helped me to control over $2 million worth of stock. I used sound trading rules and a huge amount of leverage to buy The Three

Amigos. I started to buy them when they were in safe price ranges – approximately $15.

$1.28 million – time to give Mum and Dad a gift

I bought large amounts of stock from each of the three companies, plus I day-traded each of them. By July 2003, NTES had jumped to $50.46. SINA had surged to $34.76 and SOHU had bolted to $39.74, helping our portfolio to bank some pretty good gains.

On July 10th 2003, our account was valued at $1,284,826.94 – approximately £783,000. On that same date I was fortunate enough to make a return of 16.12%, helping us make £107,543 in just one day. My brother and I used part of this gain (£50,000) to buy our dad his dream car: a Bentley Continental.

Thanks Dad – and here's your Bentley: Proud parents (Far left)
with Stephen (Left) and Paul Sutherland (Right).

Not wanting to leave Mum out, Paul and I bought her a gold, diamond-encrusted necklace. When we gave our parents their gifts they were completely caught off guard; I will never forget the looks on their faces and we all became very emotional. It took some time for the reality of what I had achieved to really sink in. To have gone from failing at almost every subject in school to being able to provide our parents with the gifts of their dreams felt incredible.

Searching for fund managers in the money flow

As well as my success with stocks, I was also doing quite well with my ISA account, which I'd started back in 1997. I managed to transfer the skills I'd learnt about the market and picking stocks into picking funds. In 2003 I invested in the *AXA Framlington Japan Fund,* which turned out to be the top performing fund in 2003, returning 91.05%. My method for picking funds involved searching for top fund managers who were in the money flow.

This helped me locate a fund that turned out to be the number one performer of the 2003–2007 bull market. It was called the *Invesco Perpetual Latin America Fund.* I also found the number three performing fund of the 2003–2007 bull market, the *Scottish Widows Latin America Fund.* Even though we invested in both these funds, the error I made was not staying in them long enough to capture the extent of their moves.

Track how you've performed by measuring against a benchmark

I've found that you have to admit your mistakes. It's very easy for an investor to focus only on their winners and forget to mention their losers – and I've had lots of losers. My take on this subject is simple: It's not about which funds or stocks you picked – it's about your overall performance. It's important that you track how you've performed by measuring against a benchmark such as the FTSE 100. If you can beat the FTSE 100 over the long term, you're doing something right.

Why I love the market

Many people want to know how many hours I've put into learning my craft. Since 1999, my best estimate is over 20,000 hours and of course, this number keeps increasing week after week. Since reading *Awaken the Giant Within* I've read close to 700 books, with many of them being books on money, investing and growing and protecting wealth. The market is a complex puzzle and I love to try to solve it.

What fascinates me about the market is that it is forever showing different sides to its personality. It always keeps you on your toes and is continually teaching you new lessons. Back in 2000, I had found a job I truly loved. I remember that in the first three or four years, I was putting in at least 70–100 hours per week on the market in the form of studying, trading, money management and regular reviews of my portfolio.

There is no way I would have done that unless I truly adored my profession. Now my working week as ISACO's Chief Investment Strategist is more in the region of 60–70 hours and my love for the market seems to strengthen each and every day. Even when on holiday, I can't keep my eyes off the market. Some people might say I'm obsessed with it, and maybe they're right.

Liquid Millionaire: **the good, the bad and the ugly**

In 2008 I wrote a book called *Liquid Millionaire.* In the book I provided evidence that suggested that, despite the fact that at the time we were experiencing a global financial crisis, a stock market boom was around the corner. People thought I was crazy.

'An up and coming boom?' they said. 'Are you nuts?'

However, I may have had the last laugh. Shortly after my book was released, the market bottomed and made a serious move to the upside, catching many investors with their trousers around their ankles. Yes, it's true: the boom I spoke about in *Liquid Millionaire* may have already begun. Have a look at this chart of the NASDAQ Composite, an index we follow very closely:

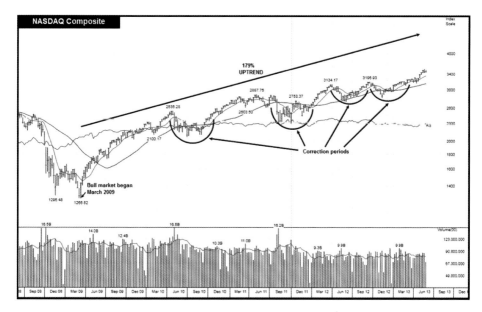

As you can see, since March 2009, even though the market has had correction periods, it has clearly been in an uptrend. By making some good decisions and with a little bit of luck, this uptrend has helped us to make double digit returns over the last five years. From December 31st 2008 to December 31st 2013, our portfolio annualised 14.5% versus the FTSE 100's 8.8%[12]. In my opinion this above 10% annual return is probably a clue that the boom I spoke about in *Liquid Millionaire* has begun.

An 86% score rating

My take is that we would not have been able to achieve these kinds of returns without the underlying strength of the present bull market. *Liquid Millionaire* has so far received 207 Amazon reviews[13] and attained an average star rating of 4.3 out of 5[14] – which is the equivalent of an 86% score rating. It was a very humbling experience to receive so many positive reviews, especially from investors who had been awakened by what they had learned.

But not everybody loved it; it was a bit too commercial and the growth expectations I set were too high, which turned some readers off. The timing of the up and coming boom I'd predicted was also slightly premature. When I wrote the book it was prior to the 2008 crash and I, like hundreds of thousands of other investors, had no idea it was coming.

We and our clients were caught out by the sharp dramatic falls and in turn had to suffer the consequences of sitting temporarily in some heavy losses. If you are one of these people who read *Liquid Millionaire* and had a negative experience, I'm so sorry. Hopefully I have learned from my mistakes and I also want to thank you for giving me a second chance.

Please, no more exams!

The former regulator, the Financial Services Authority (FSA), the UK's financial watchdog, approached us in 2009 suggesting that the personal investment service we offered might require regulation.

We initially disagreed with the FSA's opinion because we weren't offering personal recommendations or personalised advice, but in the end we realised that regulation would strengthen our company, as well as give our clients consumer protection, governance and transparency. After two arduous years, which involved Paul, Steve Todd (ISACO's Global Market Strategist) and I having to sit and pass some tough examinations set by the IFS School of Finance, the FSA gave us the stamp of approval.

Shocked by the lack of information taught

The exams the three of us sat were the same exams investment advisers take[15]. I have to say that the three of us were shocked by the lack of information taught. I know this may be hard to believe, but in the syllabus you are not taught anything about the stock market, nor are you taught anything about how to pick the best funds. You also learn nothing about stock market cycles, nothing about analysing the market and nothing about timing it.

My performance since 1997

I started investing in ISAs (ISAs used to be called Personal Equity Plans (PEPs)) in 1997 and I'm very proud of my track record. I've managed to outperform the FTSE 100 over the last 16 years by 60.2%[16], although I have to admit that I have had some rough years. My worst year was in 2008, when I made a loss of -42.3%.

My best year was 2009, when I returned 56.4%[17]. I'm also proud that, together with our clients, we have an estimated £57 million actively invested in ISAs and pensions[18]. I share my story with you to show you that anything is possible. As you've heard, I'm far from being an 'A' grade student; I was poor at maths and I'm completely self-taught. If I can beat the market and make a success with my ISA and pension investing, you can too. It just takes time, passion, effort and lots of persistence.

Now it's time to move on, my friend and take a good look at ISAs, which are an incredibly compelling tax-efficient investment shelter. Whether you are new to ISAs or whether you consider yourself an expert, I'm certain that you'll find tremendous value in this fact-filled chapter, where I'll be sharing with you how it's possible to become an ISA millionaire through the power of compound interest. I'm also going to take you through a very useful Q&A on ISAs and quickly dispel 13 ISA myths. So, let's discover all about…

2. ISAs – Aiming to become an ISA Millionaire

'The greatest appeal of investing in an ISA wrapper is that the returns go into your pocket and not the tax man's. What's not to like?'
– Holly Cook, Managing Editor of Morningstar.co.uk

ISAs are one of the best-kept investment secrets and are the UK's top tax shelter. I've been investing using ISAs since 1997 when they were previously known as PEPs. They really are a great tax-efficient solution for helping you build and preserve long-term tax-free wealth.

ISA basics

As you've probably already gathered, I'm a huge fan of ISAs. They offer a compelling combination of easy access and long-term tax advantages and can play a big part in helping you achieve your long-term financial goals. An ISA is a tried and tested way to support your retirement savings and it doesn't lock your money away as pensions do.

Did you know that ISA investing could help you build up a lump sum of £1m from which all of your income will be tax free? In fact, some ISA investors have accounts in the tens of millions[19]. Here is a quick summary of some ISA basics:

- Individual Savings Accounts (ISAs) are tax-free savings accounts
- There are two types of ISA; a stocks and shares ISA and a cash ISA
- ISAs were introduced in 1999 to replace PEPs (which were a tax free way of investing in equities) and TESSAs (which were tax free deposit accounts)
- The present annual ISA allowance is £11,880 per person (2014/15 tax year, of which up to £5,940 can be held in a cash ISA)

There aren't many ways to hide your money from the prying eyes of the taxman, but an ISA is one way of doing it. An ISA is simply a special type of savings and investment account, which is protected from tax. An ISA isn't actually an investment itself, but more of a wrapper into which you can put your money.

Any gain you make on your cash whilst it sits in the ISA wrapper will be completely tax-free. When you have built up a sizeable pot, there will be zero tax to pay on any of the money you draw as income. I'd strongly recommend that you consider the idea of investing in ISAs for life.

How to save thousands of pounds

Over the years, an ISA could save you thousands of pounds that you would otherwise have had to pay in tax. In a time when the upward pressure on tax seems to be persistent, this is doubly important. Just remember that every time tax rises, the ISA tax allowance gets even more valuable.

Of course, how much money you could save depends upon your personal circumstances. However, I believe that for many people, an ISA is one of the most generous handouts they will receive from the Chancellor.

A little history

ISAs were introduced in 1999, replacing a similar scheme called PEPs that ran from 1987 to 1999. The ISA's history is important because it shows their incredible potential.

ISA maximum contribution history – PEP and ISA history

Over the period covered in this table (page 18) you can see that it would have been possible for a couple to shelter over £400,000 from the taxman by investing the maximum PEP/ISA contribution each and every year. £400,000 tax-free is a significant amount of money, however, if this same couple had managed to achieve an annual growth rate of 7%, they would have become ISA millionaires! (See the table on page 19.)

ISA millionaire through the power of compound interest

By saving annually into a PEP/ISA, a couple adding the full allowance each year and achieving an annual growth rate of 7%, would have accumulated £1.145 million. That's exciting!

ISA maximum contribution history – PEP and ISA history

Year	ISA/PEP	Allowance 1 (£)	Allowance 2 (£) (Partner)	Total contribution per couple (£)
1987	PEP	2,400	2,400	4,800
1988	PEP	3,000	3,000	6,000
1989/90	PEP	4,800	4,800	9,600
1990/91	PEP	6,000	6,000	12,000
1991/92	PEP	9,000	9,000	18,000
1992/93	PEP	9,000	9,000	18,000
1993/94	PEP	9,000	9,000	18,000
1994/95	PEP	9,000	9,000	18,000
1995/96	PEP	9,000	9,000	18,000
1996/97	PEP	9,000	9,000	18,000
1997/98	PEP	9,000	9,000	18,000
1998/99	PEP	9,000	9,000	18,000
1999/00	ISA	7,000	7,000	14,000
2000/01	ISA	7,000	7,000	14,000
2001/02	ISA	7,000	7,000	14,000
2002/03	ISA	7,000	7,000	14,000
2003/04	ISA	7,000	7,000	14,000
2004/05	ISA	7,000	7,000	14,000
2005/06	ISA	7,000	7,000	14,000
2006/07	ISA	7,000	7,000	14,000
2007/08	ISA	7,000	7,000	14,000
2008/09	ISA	7,200	7,200	14,400
2009/10	ISA	7,200[a]/10,200[b]	7,200[a]/10,200[b]	14,400[a]/20,400[b]
2010/11	ISA	10,200	10,200	20,400
2011/12	ISA	10,680	10,680	21,360
2012/13	ISA	11,280	11,280	22,560
2013/14	ISA	11,520	11,520	23,040
Total contributions to date		**£212,280[c]**	**£212,280[c]**	**£424,560[c]**

a Applicable to those aged under 50.
b Applicable to those aged 50 and over from October 6th 2009.
c Applicable £10,200 used in calculation for 2009.

ISA millionaire through the power
of compound interest

Year	Allowance 1 (£)	Allowance 2 (Partner) (£)	Total contribution per couple (£)	@ 7% annual growth (£)
1987	2,400	2,400	4,800	5,136
1988	3,000	3,000	6,000	11,916
1989/90	4,800	4,800	9,600	23,022
1990/91	6,000	6,000	12,000	37,474
1991/92	9,000	9,000	18,000	59,357
1992/93	9,000	9,000	18,000	82,772
1993/94	9,000	9,000	18,000	107,826
1994/95	9,000	9,000	18,000	134,634
1995/96	9,000	9,000	18,000	163,318
1996/97	9,000	9,000	18,000	194,010
1997/98	9,000	9,000	18,000	226,851
1998/99	9,000	9,000	18,000	261,991
1999/00	7,000	7,000	14,000	295,310
2000/01	7,000	7,000	14,000	330,962
2001/02	7,000	7,000	14,000	369,109
2002/03	7,000	7,000	14,000	409,927
2003/04	7,000	7,000	14,000	453,602
2004/05	7,000	7,000	14,000	500,334
2005/06	7,000	7,000	14,000	550,337
2006/07	7,000	7,000	14,000	603,841
2007/08	7,000	7,000	14,000	661,090
2008/09	7,200	7,200	20,400	722,774
2009/10	7,200[a]/10,200[b]	7,200[a]/10,200[b]	20,400	795,196
2010/11	10,200	10,200	20,400	872,688
2011/12	10,680	10,680	21,360	956,631
2012/13	11,280	11,280	22,560	1,047,734
2013/14	11,520	11,520	23,040	1,145,728
Total contributions to date	**£212,280[c]**	**£212,280c**	**£424,560[c]**	

a Applicable to those aged under 50.
b Applicable to those aged 50 and over from October 6th 2009.
c Applicable £10,200 used in calculation for 2009.

How much tax will you save?

Interest from savings:

- If you pay tax at the basic rate, you pay 20% tax on your savings interest.
- If you pay tax at the highest rate, you pay 45% tax on your savings interest.

To illustrate how much tax you can save when investing in ISAs, let's imagine a pair of twins who earn identical amounts of money each and every year. Twin number 1 decides to invest without an ISA and twin number 2 decides to invest using an ISA. Each year, each twin makes identical gains of 7% on their portfolio. Twin number 1 has to pay tax on his gain and because he's a high rate taxpayer, his gain is reduced to 3.85%.

Time period invested (£1,920 per month)	Twin 1 – (no ISA) (growth at 3.85%)	Twin 2 – (ISA) (growth at 7%)
10 years	£281,395	£334,261
15 years	£468,242	£612,118
20 years	£694,682	£1,006,014
25 years	£969,105	£1,564,410
30 years	£1,301,680	£2,356,008

For illustration purposes only.

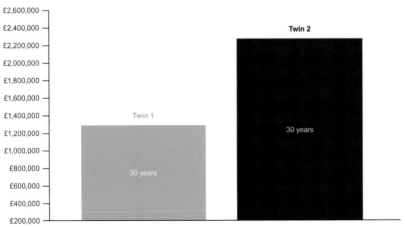

For illustration purposes only.

Twin number 2 on the other hand, keeps all of his 7% gain because his gain is protected by an ISA. Look at what happens to their trading accounts over various periods of time, assuming that both were investing £1,920 each and every month. I've used £1,920 per month in our example because it is the equivalent of the maximum that a couple could invest using an ISA for the tax year 2013/2014.

As you can see on this image, by investing over the long term using an ISA, twin 2 ends up with £2.35 million – over a million pounds more than twin 1.

Prospective clients of ours always have lots of questions regarding ISAs and I'm sure you do too, so I've put together a short Q&A covering the most frequently asked ISA-related questions. Enjoy!

Q: Who can save in an ISA?
A: Anyone who is 16 or over and a UK resident for tax purposes can save money in a tax-efficient cash ISA but to save in a stocks and shares ISA, you need to be at least 18.

Q: What types of ISAs are there?
A: There are two main types of ISAs: cash ISAs and stocks and shares ISAs.

Q: What is a cash ISA?
A: Cash ISAs usually work in the same way as normal savings accounts. You choose if you want a fixed rate account, an easy access (or instant access) account, or a regular savings account. You don't pay income tax on the interest you earn. For every £1 of interest you earn on your savings, instead of the taxman pocketing 20p (if you're a basic rate taxpayer), you get to keep it all.

Q: What is a stocks and shares ISA?

A: A stocks and shares ISA is another option open to you if you're looking to invest for at least 5–10 years. With a stocks and shares ISA, you can invest in individual stocks and shares or investment funds. Any profit you make is not subject to tax.

Q: How much can I invest?

A: Since April 6th 2014, the ISA limit has been £11,880 per person. Of this, the maximum amount you can put into a cash ISA is 50% of the annual allowance, i.e. £5,940. The remainder of your ISA limit can be invested into a stocks and shares ISA. So for example, you could put:

- The maximum £5,940 into a cash ISA and £5,940 into a stocks and shares ISA
- £2,000 into a cash ISA and £9,980 into a stocks and shares ISA
- Nothing into a cash ISA and the whole of your £11,880 ISA limit into a stocks and shares ISA

Q: When should I invest?

A: As long as you have not exceeded the current annual ISA allowance limit, you can invest in an ISA at any point during the tax year and, depending on the ISA provider, you can allocate lump sums or monthly contributions that fit around your lifestyle. The earlier and more you add to your ISA, the better. But the crucial thing to remember is that every tax year – which runs from April 6th one year to April 5th the next year – you're only allowed to invest a certain amount in an ISA. This is known as your annual ISA allowance.

Q: Where can I get an ISA?

A: You can get an ISA only by going to an HMRC approved ISA manager. I buy my ISAs from a fund supermarket but other ISA managers include: banks, building societies, financial advisers, stockbrokers and investment trust companies.

Q: Is it true that some people living in the UK are ISA millionaires?
A: Yes. Scores of people are now ISA millionaires, with £1 million-plus in tax sheltered holdings – including some who have portfolios worth £12 million[20]. However, most people in the UK are totally unaware that ISAs can help them accumulate a multi-million pound, tax-free portfolio.

The people who have become ISA millionaires have achieved this momentous task by religiously investing in ISAs over the long term. And, as each new tax-year arrives, they open up a new stocks and shares ISA to add to their existing ones. By striving for maximum capital growth each and every year, they have managed to accumulate over seven figures tax-free.

Q: What is a self-select ISA?
A: Personally I don't use these and never have. Self-select ISAs are designed for investors who want to hold individual stocks and are offered by stockbrokers and online share dealing sites. For the 2014/2015 tax year, you can buy up to £11,880 of shares through the ISA provider. Please be aware that there will be costs associated with buying and selling stocks. These will be on top of any charge for the ISA wrapper.

With stocks and shares ISAs, the old rules said that you could only invest in shares listed on 'recognised stock exchanges', however, on July 1st 2013, the Treasury announced new ISA rules and legislation that allowed investment in some small companies listed on the Alternative Investment Market (AIM).

As well as getting asked lots of questions about ISAs, we find that when we speak to clients, they have many false assumptions about what you can and can't do with ISAs. We call these 'ISA myths.' To help clarify things for you, I've put together a list of the 13 most common ones:

13 ISA Myths Dispelled

1) **ISAs are risky – FALSE**
   Did you know that an ISA isn't an investment? An ISA is a wrapper that investments are kept in to protect them from the taxman. Think of it as a shield that prevents the taxman from being able to touch your investment returns. Any risk comes from the investments that you have chosen to hold within the ISA, not from the ISA itself.

2) **With a stocks and shares ISA, you are not able to park in cash – FALSE**
   If you believe a bear market (major downtrend) has been triggered, you can move out of your fund and into the safety of cash via an ISA Cash Park. If you are ever unsure where to invest your ISA money, you can also use an ISA Cash Park.

3) **You can only open one ISA – FALSE**
   Some people mistakenly think that you can only open one ISA in your lifetime. The rules allow all adults to open up a new ISA each and every year. I've opened one every year since 1997 and remember that if you have a partner, they can also open one ISA per year – you cannot have ISAs in joint names though.

4) It's impossible to make a million with ISAs – FALSE

As reported by FT.com on October 8th 2010, scores of people are now ISA millionaires, with £1 million-plus in tax sheltered holdings – including some with portfolios worth £12 million.

5) Investing in ISAs means my money is locked up – FALSE

There is no minimum term for which the investment must be made and the tax advantages start on day one when investing in an ISA. It is always possible to gain easy access to all or part of your savings, subject to any restrictions that may be included on a particular ISA product.

6) It is best to invest in an ISA at the end of the tax year – FALSE

The tax advantages of an ISA start the day that the money is invested so, by investing earlier in the tax year, you gain more potential advantage. Since investing in ISAs back in 1997, in 95% of cases, I've added at the beginning of the year rather than the end. Remember that as soon as the year's allowance is invested, it will start to receive its tax-boost, and the longer you delay investing throughout the tax year, the smaller the boost it will get in that year.

7) If you invest in ISAs, you have to fill out a tax return – FALSE

Tax savings occur automatically within the ISA and ISAs do not have to be recorded on your tax return. You also do not need to inform HMRC (the taxman) that you have an ISA.

8) Opening an ISA is complicated – FALSE

It takes me literally minutes each year to take out a new ISA. It is a common mistake to think that opening an ISA is complicated. I can assure you that it's really easy.

9) Transferring an ISA to another manager is complicated – FALSE

ISAs can be transferred at any point to a new location, such as moving from one fund supermarket to another. Your existing platform cannot stop you from moving, but they may make a charge or force you to sell any assets to be transferred as cash. Any charges that apply will be in the terms and conditions and should be considered when shopping for an ISA.

It may also take a few weeks to complete the transfer. If you believe the delay has been unreasonable, you should contact both providers and, if you are still unhappy, complain to the Financial Ombudsman.

10) Teenagers are not allowed to own an ISA – FALSE

If you have a son or daughter who is either 16 or 17 and a UK resident they are allowed to open a cash ISA but to open a stocks and shares ISA they would need to wait until they were at least 18. Children under the age of 18 can have a Junior ISA (or its predecessor the Child Trust Fund). This means that between the ages of 16 and 18, children can hold both a Junior ISA and a Cash ISA!

11) If I move abroad I'll lose my ISAs – FALSE

It's true that you can only open an ISA if you are resident in the UK for tax purposes. If you move abroad you won't be able to open a new one or fund an existing one. You will, however, be able to keep your ISA and still get tax relief on investments held within it. Government employees, such as diplomats, are exempt from this. If you work overseas and are paid by the Government, you may open and fund an ISA.

12) **I have to invest my ISA money all in one place – FALSE**

If you choose a stocks and shares ISA you can mix up the way your money is invested by choosing a range of funds which provide exposure to different countries, sectors and markets around the world. The flexibility you have will depend on the ISA manager you choose.

13) **You are not allowed to transfer cash ISAs into stocks and shares ISAs – FALSE**

Many of my clients have moved money from a cash ISA into a stocks and shares ISA. If the cash ISA was from a previous tax year, you can move as much or a little as you like. If the cash ISA is from the current tax year, you must move all of it. You will however, be free to invest in another cash ISA, subject to the overall investment limit.

Just before we close this chapter, my friend, I wanted you to know that by using a 'Junior ISA (JISA)' you can give your child or grandchild a great start in life. In my opinion, JISAs provide an excellent tax-efficient way of saving for a child's future. For all the information you need on JISAs, go to Appendix 4, which you will find at the back of this book.

Now that you are a dynamo on the topic of ISAs, we can quickly move on to discovering about SIPPs and how they can play a part in helping you build a small fortune. You'll learn that as well as being the perfect complement to ISAs, they give you full control of your pension, provide generous tax benefits, offer flexible options for taking an income in retirement and remove the requirement to buy an annuity.

Together, let's discover…

3. SIPPs – the Smarter Way to Manage Your Pension

'Britain's workers are waking up to the pensions crisis and taking matters into their own hands by setting up and managing long-term savings plans.'
– Richard Evans

Self invested personal pensions (SIPPs) are a form of personal pension scheme approved by HMRC. Whilst they have a lot of similarities with ordinary personal pension schemes, I prefer SIPPs due to their greater flexibility and range of investment options. A SIPP is not an investment itself but simply a tax wrapper that protects the investment from personal liability for tax. Please note however that unlike ISAs, when you eventually start to take an income from your SIPP, the income taken will be taxable.

Did you know that when it comes to saving for retirement, more and more people are choosing a Self Invested Personal Pension (SIPP)? Yes, it's true, and if your goals are similar to mine, a SIPP is going to be a great way to help you achieve them. Surprisingly, SIPPs were created in 1989, yet it is only in the last five years or so that they have become popular and are now the preferred way for smart investors to manage their pension arrangements.

Let's take a look at how a SIPP works.

How a SIPP works

Contributions are invested into your chosen funds

Basic-rate tax relief is added onto each of your contributions*

The invested capital benefits from potential investment growth in a mainly tax-free environment

Benefits can be taken from the age of 55 in the form of:

• income drawdown
• annuities
• up to 25% tax-free cash

*45% tax relief is awarded, where applicable, through a SIPP holder's annual tax return.
Chart courtesy of FundsNetwork.

What are the advantages?

The four main advantages of a SIPP are:

• Tax efficiency
• Greater choice
• Better planning
• You can open a SIPP for a child

1. Tax efficiency

A SIPP is a long-term savings vehicle with great tax advantages – tax relief on contributions, tax-free growth of the fund and some of the benefits are tax-free when you draw them too. For example, from the age of 55, you can receive up to 25% of your pension fund value as a tax-free lump sum (subject to certain limits). The remaining fund value is used to provide you with an income, although there are a number of different ways in which you can achieve this.

Contributions into a SIPP offer significant tax benefits. Most importantly, you can claim tax relief on your contributions. This means that if you are a basic rate taxpayer, the Government will add another 20p into your pension for every 80p you pay in. Your maximum tax relievable contribution allowance is £50,000 but this amount will be reduced from £50,000 a year to £40,000, with effect from April 6th 2014.

If your relevant UK earnings (basically your income from employment or self-employment) are less than £50,000 per year then your maximum tax relievable SIPP contribution is 100% of these earnings rather than £50,000. If you are taking advantage of an additional 'carried forward' allowance, tax relief will also be claimed on these contributions, up to a maximum of £50,000 per contribution period. We'll talk more about the carry forward allowance a little later.

If you pay tax at a higher or additional rate, you can continue to claim any additional tax relief on the contributions made by you or by a third party on your behalf through your self assessment return on contributions up to the stated limits. Any contributions made to your SIPP after the age of 75 will not be entitled to any tax relief.

If you work for a company that contributes to your pension, make the note that employer contributions are not eligible for tax relief. The amount of pension savings you can build up over your life that benefit from tax relief is subject to an overall maximum – this is called the 'lifetime allowance'. If you build up pension savings worth more than the lifetime allowance you'll pay a tax charge on the excess. In the 2013/14 tax year the lifetime allowance is set at £1.5 million but this reduces to £1.25 million from April 6th 2014.

A £10,000 investment for just £6,000

What it could cost to invest £10,000 in a SIPP if you are a higher-rate taxpayer.

This illustration assumes income tax rates of 20% and 40%.
Please note that rates of tax may change in the future, which could affect the amount of pension tax relief you receive.
Chart courtesy of FundsNetwork.

SIPP key points

- For every 80p you pay into your pension – the Government adds another 20p
- SIPP providers will invest this tax relief some 2–6 weeks after your payment is made
- If you're a higher rate taxpayer, you may claim up to a further 20p for every £1 you contribute to your SIPP
- Your SIPP investments will grow free of tax
- The maximum tax relievable contribution allowance for the 2013/2014 tax year is £50,000
- The contribution allowance for the 2013/2014 tax year is £50,000
- You will only receive tax relief on contributions up to 100% of your relevant UK earnings if these are less than £50,000
- You can transfer from other pensions and investments into your SIPP
- You may take up to 25% of your SIPP fund as a tax-free cash lump sum after age 55

How to grow your money much faster

UK pension fund investments grow free of income tax and capital gains tax (CGT), which allows funds to grow your money faster than taxed alternatives and benefit considerably over the longer term due to the effects of compounding. Pension funds cannot reclaim the 10% tax credit on UK share dividends though.

2. Greater choice

SIPPs allow you to choose where you want to invest your pension savings. Instead of being restricted to a limited range of funds – as with some other types of pension – SIPPs offer a wide range of investments to choose from. You can also decide how much you want to invest and how often. You can even transfer in pension plans from other providers.

You can typically choose from thousands of funds run by top managers, as well as pick individual shares, bonds, gilts, unit trusts, investment trusts, exchange traded funds (ETFs), cash and commercial property (but not residential property). The precise range of investment options open to you will depend on which SIPP manager you select.

With a SIPP you are free to invest in:

- Cash & Deposit accounts (in any currency, providing they are with a UK deposit taker)
- Insurance company funds

- UK gilts
- UK shares (including shares listed on the Alternative Investment Market)
- US and European shares (stocks and shares quoted on a recognised stock exchange)
- Unquoted shares
- Bonds
- Permanent Interest Bearing Shares
- Commercial property
- Unit trusts
- Open ended investment companies (OEICs)
- Investment trusts
- Traded endowment policies
- Futures and options

3. Better planning

A SIPP provides options at retirement that can give you greater flexibility. As with other forms of pension, you can take a tax-free lump sum when you retire. There are also a number of income options to choose from, for example, you can opt for a drawdown pension if you don't want to buy an annuity.

Options at retirement

You'll probably want to keep a certain amount of freedom with your investments when reaching retirement and a SIPP's range of options can give you more flexibility and control than other pension choices. It's also good to know that you do not have to retire from work to take benefits from your SIPP. As you've heard, under current Government legislation you can begin taking benefits at any age from 55. Once you retire, a SIPP opens up several options to help you with your individual retirement needs.

Take 25% as a tax-free lump sum

Part of your pension (up to 25%) can normally be taken as a tax-free lump sum, also known as a Pension Commencement Lump Sum (PCLS). You can take a tax-free lump sum at any time from age 55, whether you then take an income from the remainder of your pension fund or not.

3 ways to take income

Whether you have taken a tax-free lump sum or not, you can draw a taxable income from your pension fund at any point from age 55. From this age you can take your benefits in stages (both income and tax-free lump sum). This is known as phased retirement. You choose how much of your current fund you use to provide benefits at each stage.

Income can be taken in the form of:

1) Drawdown pension
2) Annuity (secured pension)
3) Combination of drawdown pension and annuity

Drawdown pension: A way to keep growing your assets

Available at any time from age 55, a drawdown pension is an alternative to buying an annuity. This is something that personally appeals to me because it allows you to keep growing your pension. With a drawdown pension, you simply take a taxable income from your pension fund. There is no minimum withdrawal amount for income drawdown, so you could choose to withdraw zero income if you wish. The lower the income you take, the bigger the pension pot you leave to grow in the future.

The maximum income you can draw is calculated with reference to the equivalent level single life annuity that a person of the same age could purchase. This figure is based on rates set by the Government Actuary's Department and so is known as the GAD rate. At present, the maximum amount you can drawdown is 120% of the GAD rate, although this can be higher if you are eligible for 'Flexible Drawdown'.

Flexible Drawdown

Flexible Drawdown will allow some individuals the opportunity to withdraw as little or as much income from their pension fund as they choose, as and when they need it. To be eligible for this, you have to declare that you are already receiving a secure pension income of at least £20,000 a year and have finished saving into pensions.

Death benefits: Another reason to consider income drawdown

When you want to start drawing your pension, it is normal to consider the financial position of your spouse or civil partner, should you die before them, as well as any dependent children. Normally when buying an annuity, a choice must be made at the outset as to what proportion (if any) is to be paid on the annuitant's death. This will almost always reduce the starting pension for the surviving spouse/ civil partner.

When annuity rates are unusually low, as they are at the time of writing, this extra reduction on income is unwelcome. With an income drawdown pension, on death, the survivor can inherit 100% of the deceased's pension whilst drawing an income, or take a lump sum instead, less a tax charge.

This means a couple may happily enjoy the maximum income available at the outset, knowing that should the investor die, the survivor will not lose out. Of course it is still the case that drawing income from a fund that might be falling in value, will put the fund at risk and an investor could run out of money. So income drawdown is really only for those who are able to understand and accept this risk.

Advantages of drawdown pension

- Your pension fund remains invested
- It has the potential to still benefit from investment growth
- You can draw income directly from your assets

- You keep control of your investments
- Attractive death benefits

Risk factors

- Your pension will be exposed to the risk that investments can fall as well as rise
- When you sell your investment, you may get back less than you originally invested
- If withdrawals exceed growth, the value of your pension pot will drop

Annuity

Available at any time from age 55, a lifetime annuity converts your pension fund into taxable pension income, which will be paid to you for life. They are usually provided by insurance companies. The amount of income can be either level or increasing and is guaranteed for the rest of your life once set up. Annuities therefore may suit those who are comforted by the fact that their income will never run out.

There are a number of different types of annuity available, which allow you to take into account any requirement you may have for your spouse's pension and whether you want your income level to be linked to inflation year on year.

You should note that some annuity providers offer higher annuity rates to people who are suffering from various medical conditions or who have health limiting lifestyles. If you smoke, take medication for a medical condition, or have been hospitalised in the past five years, this may lead to a larger income from an annuity provider. Even if your pension has been set up through an insurance company you can choose to transfer out to an annuity provider of your choice using the Open Market Option (OMO).

4. Opening a SIPP for a child

It's never too early to start saving for a pension. As well as the option of investing in a Junior ISA, you can also open a SIPP for a child under 18 and get tax relief to help their retirement fund grow for longer. Many parents and grandparents use the tax benefits of SIPPs to set up pensions for their young children and grandchildren.

Did you know that less than half of Britons are actually saving for when they retire?[21] Yes, shocking but true, and yet to expect an annual retirement income of only £15,000 in today's money, children will need to have saved the equivalent of £203,528 by the time they retire.

If you start saving at 25, this means putting aside £449 a month until the age of 65. However, thanks to the power of compounding returns, you don't have to pay thousands of pounds a year to make a difference. Put away £40 a month for the first 18 years of a child's life, and, with tax relief boosting the contribution to £50 a month, it would be worth £506,064[22] when your child reaches 65, assuming 6% annual growth.

Points to remember

- Under current legislation, you can open a SIPP on behalf of a child under the age of 18
- The Government will pay basic rate income tax relief on contributions up to a maximum of £3,600 per annum, i.e. you pay £2,880 and the Government will provide £720 in tax relief
- Once the child reaches the age of 18, they can take over the management of the SIPP and make their own contributions to it, receiving tax relief in their own right

We have covered quite a bit of ground but maybe you still have some questions unanswered? If so and you fancy the idea of become an expert on SIPPs, you are going to love this very comprehensive SIPP FAQ that I've put together. By the end of it I'm pretty sure that you'll know more about SIPPs than the majority of so called 'financial experts'.

Q: What is a SIPP?

A: A Self-Invested Personal Pension (SIPP) is the name given to the type of personal pension scheme that allows individuals to make their own investment decisions from the full range of investments approved by HM Revenue and Customs (HMRC).

Q: Are SIPPs a personal pension?

A: Yes, SIPPs are a type of personal pension plan. Another subset of this type of pension is the stakeholder pension plan. SIPPs, in common with other personal pension schemes, are tax 'wrappers', allowing tax rebates on contributions in exchange for limits on accessibility.

Q: How much can I contribute to a SIPP?

A: For the current tax year 2013/14, you can pay into a SIPP a gross amount equal to your relevant earnings up to a maximum of £50,000. The tax relief rate can now be up to 45% and your SIPP contribution will receive tax relief at your top rate of tax. This is good news for higher and additional rate tax-payers who will be able to enjoy full relief on their contributions, at either 40% or 45%.

Did you know that if you have been a member of a pension scheme but have contributed less than £50,000 gross in any of the previous three tax years, you can make an additional payment into your pension? Yes, by using the carry forward rules you could make SIPP contributions up to £200,000 gross and receive up to 45% tax relief, saving you a total of £90,000 (if your taxable income is in excess of £150,000). The annual allowance falls to £40,000 from 2014/2015.

Q: How does the tax relief work?

A: The SIPP provider claims a tax refund at the basic rate (20% in tax year 2013/14) on behalf of the customer. The 20% is added to the 'pot' some 2–6 weeks after your payment is made. Higher rate and additional rate taxpayers must claim any additional tax refund through their tax return, or by otherwise contacting HMRC.

Q: What type of things can I invest into using a SIPP?

A: The exact choice of investments will depend on your SIPP manager but you can typically choose from thousands of funds, as well as pick individual shares, bonds, gilts, unit trusts, investment trusts, exchange traded funds (ETFs), cash and commercial property. The investment options for ordinary personal pensions are likely to be much narrower. Typically they will be restricted to a number of funds run by the pension provider.

Q: Who is eligible to own a SIPP?

A: Any UK resident (or individual with earnings chargeable to UK income tax) under the age of 75 can open a SIPP. In addition, Crown employees posted overseas and their spouses and civil partners can also contribute to a SIPP.

Q: What are the different types of SIPP?

A: According to Wikipedia, the pension industry has moved towards four terms in order to describe SIPP types:

(1) Deferred: This is effectively a personal pension plan in which most or all of the pension assets are held in insured pension funds.

(2) Hybrid: A hybrid SIPP is a scheme in which some of the assets must always be held in conventional, insured pension funds, with the rest being able to be 'self-invested'.

(3) Pure or Full: These types of SIPP offer unrestricted access to many types of investment.

(4) Low-cost: Low-cost SIPPs are designed for the vast majority of pension savers and offer access to thousands of funds at reduced charges but may not offer access to some of the more exotic investment options.

Q: How do I choose a SIPP?

A: SIPPs come in very different shapes and sizes and sometimes with confusing charging structures. Choosing the right SIPP can therefore be a challenging process. It is important that you end up with a SIPP that can do everything you require of it, but also offers value for money. The last thing you want is to be paying for a degree of flexibility that you will never use. The one I – and most of our clients – use is the low-cost SIPP.

Q: Can you give me a summary of the key benefits of SIPPs?

A: Yes, here are five key benefits:

(1) Like all other approved pension arrangements, they provide generous tax benefits
(2) They give you control of your pension
(3) They offer flexible options for taking an income in retirement
(4) They enable you to reduce your costs
(5) They will mean less paperwork if you consolidate existing pensions

Q: What are the tax advantages?

A: SIPPs have three significant tax advantages:

(1) Tax relief on contributions: Payments that you make to your SIPP will have basic rate income tax rebated directly into the SIPP. If you pay a higher rate of income tax, you can claim further tax relief at your marginal rate through your annual tax return.
(2) Tax-efficient returns: Any returns you make on investments inside a SIPP are free from income tax and capital gains tax (CGT).
(3) Tax-free lump sum: When you reach 55, you can start to draw pension benefits from your SIPP. You can withdraw up to 25% of the value of your pension fund tax-free, as a lump sum. All remaining withdrawals are taken as income and are subject to income tax based on your circumstances at the time.

Q: Can I open more than one SIPP?

A: Yes, if you have an existing pension arrangement – such as a company pension scheme or another SIPP or personal pension – you can still open a SIPP alongside it. You are allowed to contribute to multiple pension schemes in the same tax year, provided that your combined total contributions do not exceed the limits.

Q: How can I buy a SIPP?
A: Investing in a SIPP is very easy and you can buy one by phone, by post or by going online. SIPP providers include AJ Bell, Fidelity, Hargreaves Lansdown, James Hay, Skandia, Standard Life, Bestinvest, Alliance Trust, Sippdeal, Charles Stanley and TD Direct. I purchased mine through Fidelity.

Q: What are the risks?
A: A SIPP is just a wrapper and it is as risky as the investments you place within it.

Q: What happens if the SIPP provider goes bust?
A: Any assets you hold within a SIPP are ring-fenced and held separately from the SIPP provider. Therefore, if the SIPP provider fails, your SIPP will be safe. Any creditors will be unable to access your money and, although it will take time, and probably aggravation, you will eventually be reunited with it when it is transferred to another provider.

Q: What happens to my SIPP if/when I die?
A: In most cases, there is no inheritance tax payable on your pension when you die, since pensions are structured as a trust and sit outside your estate. However, depending on when you die (i.e. before or after age 75), whether you have taken any benefits from your pension and who will inherit your assets, there could be other taxes or charges incurred.

In theory, your pension trustees have complete discretion as to who receives your pension benefits after your death. This is necessary to ensure that these benefits are exempt from inheritance tax and if this discretion is impaired they may become taxable as part of your estate.

In practice, the trustees will consider your wishes and preference will obviously be given to your spouse and any dependants. In order to make sure your assets go to the right person, you need to complete a nomination form stating who you would like to receive the funds from your pension. If you have made no nomination and there is no obvious beneficiary, the trustees will consider the beneficiaries of your will and are likely to be influenced by this.

The FAQ is over and yes, I did say that it was pretty comprehensive. But let's not stop there. Whilst we are on the subject of SIPPs, I also wanted to dispel some 'SIPP myths'. Let's do that now.

6 SIPP Myths Dispelled

1) You have to be a high net worth investor to invest in SIPPs – FALSE

As you've heard, SIPPs were first introduced in 1989, but high costs meant that for most of the next decade they were only suitable for those with large pension funds. In recent years, however, the rise of online trading platforms has made the SIPP a cost-effective option for many investors.

2) SIPPs carry high charges – FALSE

SIPPs come in very different shapes and sizes and 'full' SIPPs can have expensive charging structures. However, more and more low-cost SIPPs are making their way into the market as middle-income investors get increasingly fed up with the poor returns on more traditional pensions. It's true that they were originally aimed at those with larger pension pots but, as charges have come down, it is now possible to run a SIPP even if you're only putting £50 per month into your pension.

3) You have to manage your pension yourself – FALSE

Although they are called 'self-invested' pensions, this does not mean that you have to make your own investments decisions. I recommend that you do make your own investment decisions, however it is possible to pay a premium to have the SIPP managed by an authorised and regulated investment adviser or stockbroker.

4) SIPPs are only for those who want a spread of sophisticated investments – FALSE

While SIPP investors can own commercial property, individual shares and traded endowment policies, and often have a choice of more than 1,000 different investment funds, not all SIPPs are designed to hold such a wide spread of investments. For example, low-cost SIPPs are aimed mainly at those who are more comfortable with a spread of collective investment funds – unit trusts or open-ended investment companies (OEICs).

5) 'SIPP approved' or 'HMRC approved' means the investment inside the SIPP is safe – FALSE

Just because a provider allows a specific investment to be held in a SIPP, it doesn't necessarily mean a significant amount of, or indeed any, due diligence has been done. The term 'SIPP approved' is used widely in connection with unregulated investments, including storage units, hotels in the UK and overseas, luxury holiday accommodation, bamboo crops, farmland in South America, renewable energy and car parks.

Unregulated investments are by their very nature higher risk than other options and the FCA (Financial Conduct Authority) are keeping a close eye on them and how they are marketed. Unregulated investments are only suitable for a minority of investors and if you do decide to invest in this way comprehensive due diligence is crucial.

Remember that using the term 'SIPP approved' or 'HMRC approved' in connection with an unregulated investment means absolutely nothing. There is no organisation which checks SIPP investments and provides them with a stamp of approval. The regulator certainly doesn't approve them, after all these are unregulated investments. Personally, I wouldn't touch unregulated investments with a barge pole.

6) You can't carry forward unused annual allowances – FALSE
At the time of writing, it is possible to carry forward any unused annual allowances. Carry forward was a rule introduced in the 2011/12 tax year that allows you to use any leftover annual allowances from the last three tax years and apply them in the current tax year to top up your pension and receive tax relief on the additional contributions.

The allowance for each year is currently £50,000. That works out as a maximum of £150,000 for the previous three years and an additional £50,000 for the current year. However, you would need to have at least this level of income, since your maximum contribution is limited to 100% of your earnings.

Okay my friend, seeing as you are now a fully fledged 'SIPP expert', we can move on to discovering about fund supermarkets and all the costs connected to investing. In the next chapter you're going to learn how fund supermarkets can provide you with an excellent investment platform to buy and manage funds at low cost. We are also going to look at the different types of fund supermarkets and I'm going to give you some great tips on what to look for when selecting one.

Let me ask you a question. Are you interested in reducing the costs associated with investing? I assume you are and that's great because we'll also be exploring the total cost of fund investing. You're going to learn all the costs involved with fund investing using a supermarket, plus the underhand tactics employed by the investment industry that you need to be aware of. We are also going to delve into the fees and charges associated with investing in funds and how to dramatically reduce them. Yes, it's time to learn all you need to know about…

4: Charges, Fees and Fund Supermarkets

'Investors must know what they're paying for, and the headwinds they have to overcome.'
– Matthew Vincent, FT Columnist

Before we look at fees and charges and all the associated costs that are involved with investing in funds, we are going to start by looking at platforms. A trading platform is a method of buying, selling and holding investments at a considerable discount. Some platforms give the appearance of being free, but are in fact earning money from rebates paid to them from the fund companies.

Two types of trading platform

There are two types of trading platform: the 'whole of market' platform and the 'fund supermarket'. Whole of market platforms are what many financial advisors use on behalf of their clients and have a greater choice of investments. They enable the investor to buy any fund traded in the UK, including institutional funds. Whole of market platforms are aimed at the professional investor and the independent financial adviser (IFA), and require rather more knowledge to operate.

Fund supermarkets; an easy way to invest in funds at low cost

Fund supermarkets are websites which provide an easy way of investing in collective investment funds. Funds are the investment you use in combination with ISAs, a SIPP or both. By the way, if you are new to funds, you'll learn all you need to know when we look at them in more depth in the next chapter.

Fund supermarkets provide access to a variety of funds from different fund families and allow you to buy a variety of products from one central location i.e. the website. The primary benefit of a fund supermarket is simplicity: you can buy funds from different fund families and receive all your statements in a single report. Fund supermarkets were pioneered in America and first introduced to the UK investor at the end of 1999.

Among the first to appear were Fidelity's FundsNetwork in 2000, and this is the one my clients and I use. Since then, the choice of supermarkets has become much larger. Differences in fund supermarkets can be found in the number of funds they offer, services and functionality. Most of them offer no advice, although many provide research tools to help you decide which funds to invest in.

Benefit from substantial discounts

Many fund supermarkets do offer substantial discounts on the initial charge (or set up charge) of a fund. Initial charges for direct investment with the management group could be as high as 5.5%, whereas some fund supermarkets will reduce this cost to 0%. The majority of fund supermarkets offer direct funds such as unit trusts and OEICs, offshore or onshore investment bonds and saving accounts such as Individual Savings Accounts (ISAs); very few include investment trusts in their range.

Fund supermarkets aimed at private investors

Fidelity FundsNetwork (https://www.fidelity.co.uk) is aimed at private investors and has a huge presence in the market. As I just mentioned, FundsNetwork is the supermarket I personally use. As part of the service we offer, our clients benefit from paying 0% initial charges on more than 1200 funds (a typical saving of 3–5.5%) and enjoy unlimited fund switching for 0% throughout the year. The reason I share this with you is to illustrate that by going through an adviser, you may get a better deal than going direct to the fund supermarket.

With Fidelity being the current market leader, their service being excellent and having personally invested with them since 1997, I can give them my firm stamp of approval. This however, is not to say that Fidelity is the best supermarket or the cheapest. You may find better offers at other supermarkets, so it's always worth your while searching the net before you make your ultimate decision about which one you plan to use.

The fund supermarkets aimed at individual investors include:

Fidelity FundsNetwork (https://www.fidelity.co.uk),
Cavendish Online, a fund supermarket powered by FundsNetwork (http://www.cavendishonline.co.uk),

Skandia (http://www2.skandia.co.uk/),
Interactive Investor (http://www.iii.co.uk/),
Hargreaves Lansdown (http://www.hl.co.uk/)
and Alliance Trust Savings (http://www.alliancetrustsavings.co.uk/).

Supermarkets for IFAs and wealth managers

Fidelity's FundsNetwork (https://www.fidelity.co.uk/adviserservices/default.page) and Cofunds (https://www.cofunds.co.uk/) allow independent financial advisers (IFAs) and wealth managers to take their website and brand it as their own. This means that the adviser's customer can access the same facilities and take advantage of the funds and tools (such as an account management tool) offered through the supermarket. There are also 'whole of market' platforms that are specifically geared up for IFAs and wealth managers who wish to manage their clients' investments for them.

These include:

Ascentric (http://www.ascentric.co.uk),
Nucleus (http://www.nucleusfinancial.com/),
Transact (https://www.transact-online.co.uk/),
AXA Elevate (http://www.axawealth.co.uk/adviser/elevate-platform)
and Standard Life's Adviserzone
(https://www.adviserzone.com/adviser/public/adviserzone/home).

How much are you paying for your investments?

If you are keen to pay the lowest fees when searching for a suitable fund supermarket, one website that may prove useful is Rplan (http://www.rplan.co.uk/), a fund platform with a focus on charges. The site aims to educate you on the various fees you are likely to pay on funds. It claims to be the only provider in the UK that shows you how much you will pay for your investments before you buy them.

Rplan has a cost comparison tool that enables its customers and potential customers to compare Rplan against other fund platforms and discount brokers on initial charges, ongoing charges, dealing charges and any other charges. The tool is available to all, free of charge, at http://www.rplan.co.uk/compare. It shows that, based on a basket of popular funds, some of the biggest name platforms in the UK are in fact the most expensive.

You can use Rplan's cost comparison tool to type in different investment amounts over various time periods. Remember however, that no two supermarkets are the same and sometimes that means unfair comparisons. Costs do matter but you should never underestimate other key factors, such as financial strength, choice of funds, ease of use, customer service, and whether the company is seen as a leader in its field.

Smoke and mirrors to mislead customers

2012 was the year in which fund charges became the all important issue facing the industry. Several industry campaigns were launched to point out the devastating effects of charges, notably the True and Fair Campaign (http://www.trueandfaircampaign.com/) which argues that the investment industry has been using smoke and mirrors to mislead customers on charges for too long.

In a 32-page report, 'Promoting Trust and Transparency in the UK Investment Industry', SCM Private reported that only 19% of investors know what they pay in fund management fees[23]. The survey revealed that 89% of savers and investors would like fund managers to make known a full breakdown of fees, and 83% want to know where their money is being invested.

The issues of hidden fees, lack of clarity and confusing language have unfortunately affected the investment industry for the past decade. Sadly, this means that the odds are stacked against investors being able to make informed and competitive decisions regarding their investments.

Charges and fees can be a minefield

Charges have an impact on your returns, especially when you invest for the long-term. Just a small deviation in your return over a long period can make an enormous difference. That's why it's vitally important that you understand what you are being charged when investing in funds.

Even though investment companies are being forced to be more transparent, in my opinion, enough is still not being done.

Passive funds that track a stock market index normally have relatively low charges but some have charges just as high as actively managed funds, which is daylight robbery. Plus, with trackers, because of charges and tracking error, you are guaranteed to *underperform* the index you are tracking. Actively managed funds tend to have higher fees and charges due to investment expertise and extensive research, and if you choose wisely and manage your portfolio effectively, you may outperform the market.

Here is a list of possible charges incurred:

Initial charge: An initial charge can be 5.5% or more, especially if you buy direct from the fund management company. However, this initial charge can be dramatically reduced or completely removed by buying through a fund supermarket.

Annual Management Charge (AMC): All actively-managed funds carry an Annual Management Charge (AMC). This is a percentage that's deducted from your investment account every year. The charge is automatically reflected in the fund's price, so you may not even notice it. Almost all companies you buy your funds from will keep a substantial share of this charge. We'll talk more about this charge later.

Platform fee (sometimes called the service fee): This is generally 0.25% and forms part of the AMC. As from April 6th 2014, this fee will be removed from the AMC and will appear as a separate charge on your statement.

Total expense ratio (TER): This is the charge I focus on most and I recommend you do too. The TER is a much better indication of a fund's cost than the AMC. It is a total of the AMC, service fees, registrar charges and fund expenses associated with the management of the fund. The TER has recently been replaced with the term 'ongoing charges'.

According to the fund tracker Lipper, the total expense ratios in most European countries are as much as 50 to 100 basis points higher than the US, which in 2012, had average TERs of just 0.77%[24]. You can find the TER in the Key Investor Information Document (KIID).

Switching fee: If you switch money from one fund to another you will normally have a switching fee to pay and you may also have to pay the initial charge for the new fund that you switch into.

Portfolio transactional cost: In May 2012, the Investment Management Association (IMA) looked at the effect of transaction costs on the total costs of unit trusts. For the top 15 largest active UK funds, transaction costs (commissions and taxes) added 0.38% to the total cost of the fund. For a FTSE 100 tracker, the increase was only 0.09%. So, for a unit trust with an annual management charge of 1.5% and a TER of 1.7%, a truer cost is around 2.08%. Performance fees and exit charges on some funds would add on more cost.

Bid-offer spread: If you look in the financial press you'll see that there are two prices quoted for some funds; a price to buy, the offer price, and a price to sell, the bid price. You'll learn more about this in the next chapter.

Exit fees: Some fund companies and some supermarkets charge exit fees when you sell.

Performance Fees: You sometimes have to pay performance fees on funds you purchase. Analysts at Lipper, calculate that there are now 91 funds[25] with performance fees, up from just 58 at the end of 2009. About two-thirds of these can charge performance fees if the fund loses money but outperforms a falling index.

What is the total cost of owning a fund?

With all the possible charges to consider, how can we simplify this? FundsNetwork analysed the most widely held funds[26] and found that the average total cost of owning a typical actively-managed £10,000 investment was £16.67 per month or £200 a year. That means, if you purchase a typical actively managed fund, they believe you should expect the charges to total about 2% per year.

Here's Fidelity's breakdown of the total cost of owning an actively managed fund:

Annual Management Charge (AMC):	0.75%
Administration charges:	0.14%
Cost of advice:	0.50%
Platform charge:	0.25%
Dealing costs:	0.36%
Total annual charges:	2.0%

Fidelity also calculated that the typical total annual charges for a low cost active fund would be approximately 1.45% per year and for a tracker fund, 0.39% per year.

Charges made simple

Charges and fees can seriously eat into your returns. When you fail to achieve adequate growth, you run the risk of your wealth decreasing and if this happens during your retirement, it can have terrible consequences. To help increase the probability that this doesn't happen to you, I'm now going to attempt to simplify charges. Throughout your investment career, you have to be aware of who is charging you and what the charge is for.

As you've heard previously, there are many different ways that you can be charged when investing in funds and so I suggest you always ask your adviser (if you have one) and your platform provider (or broker), what they are charging you. Clarify the amount being charged, what the charge is for, how it is charged and whether it will appear on your statement.

Some fees called 'explicit charges' will appear on your statements but others, 'implicit charges' won't. Make sure you get verification in writing. I also recommend that you look at the terms and conditions to do a cross check. My guess is that what you think you are getting charged and what you are actually getting charged are two entirely different amounts.

When you add up all the costs together and factor in inflation, my estimate is that you would probably need to make a return of approximately 6% per year just to break even! Shocked? Yes, I was too when I first discovered the real cost of investing. Discovering these truths reminded me why most investors need to set their aims higher. My belief is that if investors knew the actual costs associated with investing, the majority would increase their return targets.

Charges before January 1st 2013

On January 1st 2013, new rules came into effect which have changed the way financial advisory companies operate. Known as the Retail

Distribution Review (RDR), the objective is to raise professional standards in the industry, introduce greater clarity between the different types of service available and make the cost of advice very clear. The RDR is a key part of the Financial Conduct Authority's (FCA) consumer protection strategy.

The idea behind it is that you'll have more confidence and trust if you do decide to seek retirement and investment planning advice from a qualified adviser. Investors want to know if they were being charged fairly and prior to January 1st 2013, if you were investing in actively managed funds, a minimum of 1.5% was taken directly out of your investment account. This 1.5% is called the Annual Management Charge, or AMC for short.

Here's the breakdown of the 1.5% AMC and how it was distributed pre January 1st 2013:

- The product provider would take 0.75% (Schroder, Jupiter, Invesco etc)
- 0.25% would go to the platform provider (Fidelity, Hargreaves Lansdown, etc)
- 0.5% would be paid to the financial adviser

Since January 1st 2013, the 0.5% that typically went to the adviser has been banned. This was known as 'trail commission'. Before January 1st 2013, when you traded on a platform, if you didn't assign a person or company as your adviser, the platform provider would, by default, assign themselves as your adviser and this would mean that they could pocket the 0.5% trail. At the time of writing, this practice still goes on. That means in some cases, the platform provider and the product provider split the 1.5% down the middle.

Half the AMC would go to the fund company and the other half would go to the platform provider. I urge you to explore a handful of the fund supermarkets' terms and conditions because what I found when I took a closer look was that the majority of the revenue these companies make is created from the AMC. When I started to dig, I discovered that some platform companies state in their terms and conditions that they 'may also receive reasonable gifts from product providers', which to me sounds a little suspicious.

Charges after January 1ˢᵗ 2013

Post RDR, the majority of fund companies are still charging 0.75% to invest in their actively managed fund range, even though it may appear at first glance that they have slashed their prices. New 'unbundled' share classes have been created to replace the old style 'bundled'. With the bundled share class, if you peeled back the layers of the AMC, you'd see the 0.75% fund manager fee, the 0.25% platform fee and the 0.5% trail commission. With the new unbundled versions, the 0.5% trail has been stripped out and in some cases so has the 0.25% platform fee.

This is why you'll find the majority of these new share classes priced with an AMC of 0.75%. This new share class comes with fancy names such as commission-free, clean, unbundled and super clean. When you invest in these new types of share classes, the platform provider will charge you an 'explicit' annual platform fee which will probably be 0.25%. The key lesson here is that, whether you are investing in a bundled share class or unbundled, the fund company will still be getting their 0.75% and the platform provider will still be getting their 0.25%.

3 Categories of Charges

Let's start to break these charges down and keep things simple by putting them into three categories:

1) Fund charges
2) Platform charges
3) Advisory charges

1) Fund charges

Fund charges are also known as product charges. Fund companies charge one-off fees (e.g. the initial fee) and ongoing fees (e.g. the AMC). When you invest in a fund, the fund company will always charge you an ongoing annual fee. Whether the fund company is Schroder, Jupiter, Invesco, or any of the hundreds of other investment houses, they will all charge an annual fee. This fee is an implicit charge, meaning it's invisible and does not appear on your statement.

This charge is masked from your view and taken directly out of your investment account. A tiny amount will be removed from your account on an almost daily basis and it's impossible to see or know how much has been deducted. Because it's so small, you don't even notice that it's been taken. It is a strange fact and one heck of a coincidence that almost all the UK fund management companies charge exactly the same AMC for their actively managed fund range.

This is typically 0.75%. I remember seeing Alan Miller from SCM Private on CNBC touching on this point and mentioning that there was an almost 'cartel' feel about what's going on. Alan said that across the pond the American fund companies have varying charges for their AMCs but in the UK all of them charge the same. That is interesting. The thing that really bothers me is that fund companies, platform companies and fund supermarkets have all failed to explain this invisible annual ongoing fee to people like you and me.

It appears that they've purposely locked this secret away from the private investor community and for countless years got away with it. I learned how this covert fee was taken during my research of platforms and fund companies. I found that on every occasion, the details about how this charge gets deducted is always in small print and usually buried deep in the companies' terms and conditions.

It's also in language that is unclear and vague. As well as being charged a 0.75% annual management charge, there are other ongoing fees to be aware of. For example, some funds with 'absolute return' in the title operate like a hedge fund, which means they use both long and short trading strategies, with the aim of making a positive return for the investor in both up and down markets.

This sounds good in theory but I am yet to be compelled to invest in one. Hedge funds charge a 20% performance fee and so do absolute return funds. Some funds without the term 'absolute return' in the title also charge a performance fee. You can quickly check whether a fund charges a performance fee by looking at the fund's Key Investor Information Document (KIID).

There are also other ongoing fees to be aware of, such as trustee fees, auditor fees, portfolio transactional costs, stamp duty reserve taxes and transfer taxes which, when bundled together, can bump up the annual ongoing charge by a further 1%. Fund companies also charge one-off fees, such as entry and exit fees.

Entry fees are also known as initial charges and often these can be as high as 7.5%. Always check the KIID to check what the entry and exit fees are because I've seen funds with really low TERs with a whopping 7.5% entry charge[27]. The good news is that some funds' initial fees can often be dramatically reduced – sometimes to zero – if you buy smartly through a fund supermarket.

Fund exit fees can be as high as 5% but can mostly be avoided if you invest on the right platform. However, you have to be careful because some funds will charge you an exit fee if you invest in them for less than 90 days. An investor who uses a stop loss strategy when investing in funds could get clobbered with a hefty exit fee should they get stopped out within the 90-day penalty period. Make a mental note that when it comes to the fund costs and charges, it's always best to confirm what you are getting charged by checking the fund's KIID.

2) Platform charges

Whether you are on Fidelity's FundsNetwork, Hargreaves Lansdown's Vantage or any of the many other supermarket platforms, you will be getting charged a fee. You may think it's free to invest on a fund supermarket platform but it isn't. Platforms come with annual fees and one-off fees.

Annual charges are typically 0.25% and pre the RDR, this fee was implicit, meaning it was hidden and did not appear on your statements. In the past, many platform providers and brokers have kept the details of this fee in their terms and conditions. This means that for years they've managed to fool the majority of investors into thinking that investing on their platform was free.

Just like the annual fee that the fund company charges you, this 0.25% annual fee has been taken directly out of your account every time the investments you own update for the day. Phase 2 of the RDR (which begins on April 6th 2014) is banning this practice, which means that the platform charge will become an explicit fee and will appear on your statement.

Some platforms have acted early and started to make this charge explicit prior to the April 6th 2014 deadline. As well as annual fees, there are one-off fees such as dealing charges and these do appear on your statements. When you make a switch out of a fund you own, a charge may be levied. Dealing in funds is typically 0.25% per trade. If you make four switches to your total portfolio in a year, this would add a further 1% to the total cost of your investing.

3) Advisory charges

In the post RDR world, advisory charges have become explicit, which means you now have total transparency and you will know exactly what you are getting charged by your advisor. Advisers can charge initial fees, ongoing fees and specified fees. Initial fees can be charged at a fixed amount or at a percentage of your portfolio. Ongoing fees or 'fees for service' may be a fixed amount but are more likely to be a fee that represents a percentage of your portfolio value.

This could be anything from 0.1% to 3% per year. An ongoing service charge should reflect the level of service given and if a percentage is charged, it will normally be on a sliding scale. For example, an investor with a portfolio value of less than £50,000 could be charged 3% per year but an investor with over £1 million might be charged 0.5% or less. Specified fees are a fixed amount agreed between you and your adviser, normally for one-off tasks.

Rebates and loyalty bonuses

You've discovered that the bundled share classes have 0.5% trail commission factored into their annual charges and you now know that trail commission has been banned. The big question is what is happening to the 0.5% trail? Who is getting it? I discovered that some platform providers give back all of the trail and others give part of it back.

Some are keeping it all. This giving back of the trail is called a rebate, or a unit rebate and some companies call it a loyalty bonus. At the time of writing, bundled share classes are still around and I expect that they will be around for a while, which means rebates and loyalty bonuses could remain for some time.

Eventually, the bundled share class is likely to get phased out and replaced by the new kid on the block; the clean share class. With ISAs and collectives, the rebate is normally in the form of units. However, with SIPPs, this rebate is normally in cash, paid directly into the investor's SIPP cash account. If you invest outside tax shelters like stocks and shares ISAs and SIPPs, rebates and loyalty bonuses are taxed as income.

Hidden charges taken directly from your investment account

Pre 2013, fund companies were charging investors a minimum of 0.75% for the privilege of investing in their funds. This charge was hidden and undetectable and taken from investors' accounts every time the fund updated its price. Post 2013, these same fund companies are still charging around 0.75% to invest in their funds and the charge remains hidden to this day.

Whether you are investing in a bundled share class, unbundled, clean, completely clean or super clean, most fund companies are charging the same as they used to charge, which is 0.75%. Platform providers have been charging investors approximately 0.25% for the opportunity to trade on their platform.

In most cases this 0.25% was a hidden charge and taken directly from your investment account. From April 6th 2014, this practice will be banned and will become an explicit charge, which means that it will appear on your statements. This makes the charge transparent and allows investors to compare platform providers' charges like for like. Pre 2013, advisers were able to take a 0.5% annual trail commission.

This practice has since been banned, meaning that all advisory fees will now appear on your statements. This tells you that the industry is now much more transparent than it used to be thanks to the Financial Services Authority (FSA) and the Financial Conduct Authority (FCA). It's worth remembering that fund companies and platform providers want you and I to believe that we are now getting a better deal. The truth is, we are still paying the same – the fund company still gets their 0.75% and the platform provider still gets their 0.25%.

Until the day that all charges become explicit, it is going to be impossible to know exactly what amount is being deducted from your account.

A 0% share class

We were encouraged by an article written by Kyle Cladwell on June 17th 2013 called 'Fund groups eye 0% share classes as alternative to 'super clean''. Kyle reported that some of the UK's largest fund houses are considering launching retail share classes with a 0% AMC rather than provide platforms with 'super clean' alternatives.

This move would pave the way for confidential fee arrangements more commonly seen in the institutional space. A 0% share class would introduce an institutional-style pricing arrangement across the retail market. Instead of collecting a share of the AMC, fund groups would invoice platforms using investment management agreements, having pre-agreed a price.

Although platforms would be given 0% share classes, the end investor would be charged an overall annual fee for each fund in the same way they are now. Only this overall cost would be made public. This means you would see the charge on your statements instead of it being hidden – like it is at the moment.

Total Provider Cost (TPC) + Total Cost of Investment (TCI)

We fully support the philosophy of the True and Fair Campaign, which suggests that the investment industry needs to change.

The headline on their website (http://www.trueandfaircampaign .com/) shouts:

> *It's time for transparency, it's time to see what we are investing in and it's time for a change.*

Their manifesto states:

We call on the Government, Parliament and regulators to require that the UK investment management industry provide every prospective customer with:

- A guarantee of 100% transparency as to where their money is invested
- A guarantee of 100% transparency as to the full underlying costs of investments
- A code and labelling scheme, which ensures consumers are provided with product information in a consistent, unified and understandable format

One of their ideas that we really like is to give investors the 'Total Provider Cost' (TPC) and the 'Total Cost of Investment' (TCI).

The TPC would display the cost of items such as:

- Initial charge

- Annual Management Charge (AMC)
- Total expense ratio (TER)
- Other expenses (e.g. interest, stamp duty, audit, custody, depository and trustee fees)
- Fund administration charge (also referred to as the service fee)
- Fund expenses
- Performance fee
- Dealing costs/transactional costs
- Bid-offer spread
- Dilution levy

The TCI would display the cost of items such as:

- Platform fees
- Entry/exit costs
- Switching fees
- Advisor fees/rebates

In May 2013, the True and Fair Campaign launched a calculator that estimates and compares your likely 'Total Cost of Investing', in pounds and pence, as well as a %. It helps to identify all costs along the investment chain. We think it's great and you can take a look by going to: http://www.trueandfaircalculator.com/index

My friend, you should now be fully up to speed with charges, fees and fund supermarkets. I'd be very surprised if you weren't enlightened by some of the information I shared with you in this chapter, especially the material regarding hidden charges. Now it's time for me to share with you exactly what a fund is, the countless benefits of fund investing, the risks, types of funds and the key differences between managed funds and trackers. Let's take a look at...

5: A Quick Guide to Investment Funds

*'I have always believed that you cannot start to understand a
fund without a solid appreciation of the investment team and its
organisation as a business.'*
– Jerome de Lavenere Lussan, author of *Financial Times Guide to
Investing in Funds*

We'll start with the most basic of questions: *What is a fund?* A fund
is a form of collective investment that lets you invest indirectly in
company shares or other types of investments. The fund pools
together the money from many individuals to give you a stake in a
ready-made portfolio.

The fund manager manages the fund on a daily basis and uses the
pooled money to invest in a range of investments, such as shares,
with the aim of delivering growth, income or a mix of both, in line
with the fund's aim or objective. The fund manager is the person
who decides where the fund's money should be invested.

The many benefits of fund investing

The benefits are numerous. On your behalf, the fund manager watches
the markets daily and judges the best time to buy or sell. There are

thousands of funds available, so there should be one that matches your goals and the level of risk you're comfortable with. You can also choose whether you want a fund that gives you a regular income or one that reinvests the income to deliver long-term growth.

Some funds offer a mix of growth and income. When you invest in a fund your risk is spread, which means that your investment does not depend too heavily on the fortunes of individual companies. In my opinion, it's much more risky to invest in individual shares because when you get it wrong it can have disastrous consequences, especially when you are using a large amount of capital.

For example, one of my clients invested heavily in an American insurance company back in 2008 after it was recommended to him by a well known financial services company. Nine months after purchase, the company he bought collapsed and the client ended up losing hundreds of thousands of pounds.

Fund investing made easier

Funds benefit from tax-efficiencies. For example, you can do what I do and put funds into an investment ISA or personal pension plan such as a SIPP and benefit from the tax advantages. When you invest in funds, you also benefit from reduced dealing costs.

If you want to buy a range of different investments yourself, you might only be able to invest a small sum in each. This means that dealing costs could eat into your profits. By pooling your money with many others in the fund, the dealing costs will be spread and will have a much smaller impact on each individual.

The risks to be aware of

There are a number of risks that you need to be comfortable with. You should consider that the value of your investment and the income it produces can go down as well as up, so you could get back less than you invested. Funds are designed to be held for the medium or long term (usually 5–10 years). If you sell earlier you increase the risk that you will lose money, although losses could occur whenever you sell.

It's good to know that UK authorised funds, their managers and their trustees/depositaries are authorised by the Financial Conduct Authority (FCA) and therefore, governed by strict regulations. If the fund management company goes bust, your investment in the fund or funds you own legally belong to you and not the manager. You'll probably be comforted to know that fund assets are held in trust for you and kept separate from the manager.

Your choice of funds

The two main types of fund are:
- Investment funds: unit trusts and OEICs
- Investment trusts

Investment funds: unit trusts and OEICs

OEICs are my recommended choice because they are single priced. This means shares in the fund are both bought and sold at the same price. Unit trusts however have what's known as a 'spread' between the buy and sell price.

This means that as soon as you buy, you have to make a few percentage points just to get back to where you were when you bought. For example, the buy price on the day you buy is 105 and the sell price is 100. In this example, there is a 5% spread, which means the fund has to gain 5% just to get to the price you paid. This is a rip off and is the main reason I prefer single priced OEICs.

If you decide to buy a unit trust you will always pay the offer price. If you sell units, they will be sold at the bid price.

- Offer price (also known as the buying price)
- Bid price (also known as the selling price)

The spread between the bid and the offer is typically 5–6% in most unit trusts. This spread is similar to what you get when buying illiquid individual shares and can have a huge negative impact on your overall returns.

Investment trusts

Investment trusts pool investors' money just like unit trusts and OEICs. And, like unit trusts and OEICs, they are professionally managed and diversify your risk by investing in a wide range of companies. But they do have some differences. The main one is that the price or market value of shares held in an investment trust may not be the same as the value of the investment trust's assets. This means that you do not buy in or sell out at prices that directly reflects the value of the trust's assets due to premiums and discounts.

Shares in an investment trust company are bought and sold on the stock market. If an investment trust's shares are in demand, its price rises to a premium however, if there are more sellers than buyers, the price can fall to a discount. Buying at a discount can psychologically appear to be a good deal but there are two things to take into account here. Firstly, investment trusts trade at a discount for a reason and generally it's due to lack of demand.

This could be because the sector/country/area that the trust invests in has fallen out of favour, or it could be because investors think that the trust manager is incompetent. The second thing to be aware of is that when a trust is trading at a discount, the discount could widen even further.

This means that although discounts may seem to present an excellent opportunity, they can be bad for you if the discount increases during the time you hold the shares. Because investment trusts are traded on a stock exchange, it means you will also have 0.5% stamp duty to pay every time you place a trade. If you frequently trade investment trusts, these trading costs can add up and eat into your returns.

There will also be a spread between the buying and selling price. This is generally 1–2% but for less frequently traded trusts, it can be 5–10%. They are also not as cheap as claimed and use gearing, which is borrowed money to invest. This borrowing comes with a hefty charge to you the investor. Some trusts charge an annual administration fee (which can be as much as 1%) and many charge a performance fee, which can also nibble away at your returns.

The annual charges of investment trusts are not as transparent as they should be. For example, the average TER of a trust is approximately

0.95%. However, this fairly low TER is a bit of a smokescreen because it ignores other significant costs such as interest payments on borrowings, tax on fund performance and performance fees – which can be ridiculously high. Generally, you should avoid any investments that charge performance fees.

One thing that really bothers countless investors (including me) about performance fees is when they are charged for 'performance' even though the trust has made a negative return for the year. Phil Oakley at MoneyWeek wrote a great article called, *'We like investment trusts but they need to cut their fees'*[28].

Phil discovered that the average published TER of 32 investment trusts was 0.94%. However after the other significant costs were factored in, the true TER averaged at 1.71%. Because of the many negatives that come with investment trusts, I have personally never invested in one and probably never will.

What style of fund suits you?

Some funds that aim for higher returns over the long term are called adventurous funds. This usually means that the fund could reap attractive returns over the long term but will be volatile in the short term. However, a fund adopting a more cautious approach may see a lower return over the long term than its adventurous neighbour but is less volatile in the short term. Even though they're not suited for everybody, I really like adventurous funds due to my risk profile and very long-term investment horizon.

Continuing with the theme of investment style, some funds invest in small companies. This normally implies that they are higher risk. When choosing between funds that invest in small, medium or large companies, I normally choose large because larger companies have proved themselves and are more established than their medium and smaller counterparts.

Managed funds and trackers

Managed funds do not track a particular index and instead aim to outperform one. The fund manager invests in different companies that are carefully selected according to the fund's brief. A passive fund or index tracker is designed to replicate the performance of an index. Index tracker funds attempt to track the movement of a stock market index. This means that your investment aims to replicate the companies listed in a particular index – the FTSE 100, for example.

Because of charges, cash drag, and the other factors, there will always be a difference between the performance of the exchange traded fund (ETF) and the investment it tracks. This difference is referred to as the 'tracking error'. Tracking error occurs on index tracker funds as well as ETFs. ETFs are traded on a stock exchange, which means you'll have 0.5% stamp duty to pay every time you make a trade.

You'll also have the bid-offer spread to pay and if the fund is illiquid, the spread could be 5–10%. Even though index tracker funds and ETFs publish lower annual charges (TERs) when compared to actively managed funds, 95% of the funds I use for my ISA and SIPP are actively managed.

Active versus passive investment

Active managers can deliver high returns, but picking the right one is hard to do. If you've not had much success with picking good funds in the past, help is at hand. I'm going to show you in the next chapter exactly what I look for when searching for a good fund to invest in. Your choice of actively managed funds heavily outweighs passive funds. There are over 2,000 actively managed funds and only 70 passive funds listed by the Investment Management Association.

Actively managed investment funds are run by a professional fund manager who makes all the investment decisions. They have extensive access to research in different markets and sectors and often meet with companies to analyse and assess their prospects before making a decision to invest. An actively managed fund can offer you the potential for much higher returns than a particular market is already providing, due to a professional manager tactically managing your money.

The challenge however, with actively managed funds, is that not many fund managers beat the stock market to which their investment selection is linked. For example, analysis of the UK All Companies sector at the end of 2010[29] showed that only 24% of actively managed funds managed to beat the benchmark stock market (the FTSE All-Share) over the past decade.

This means that there's a 76% chance you could end up with a fund that is not delivering you the return you could get by simply tracking the index with a passive fund. As such, finding talented managers is of paramount importance. Passive investment funds simply track a market, and charge far less in comparison. However, passive funds also have their problems, with many of them not mirroring their benchmark and underperforming it by a wide margin.

Joshua Ausden, Editor at FE Trustnet wrote a wonderful article[30] showing that some FTSE 100 trackers underperform their benchmarks by over 2% per year, resulting in them underperforming their benchmark over a 10 year period by a whopping 41.14%. Jason Britton, formerly a fund manager at T Bailey, wrote a piece for FT.com called 'Trackers are Crackers'[31] which stated that, over a 15 year time span, the FTSE ALL-Share Index tracker funds have, on average, underperformed the index by 1.9% a year.

Over 15 years, that average underperformance compounds to 24.7%. Jason explains why these trackers underperform: 'There are two areas where performance is lost: fees, which can be as high as 1.25% a year; and the "tracking error" experienced by these funds.'

The benefits of active management

If you pick the right actively managed fund, you could make much more money than by simply investing in a tracker fund or ETF. There are some very skilled managers, who have built up reputations of consistent high returns and can be worth the fees you pay for them. The key, as you'll see in the next chapter, is to focus on star-performing managers.

Are higher fees for active management justified?

Let me ask you a question. If you opted for actively managed funds, paid a bit extra (about 1% higher than passive funds) and managed to achieve market beating returns, would paying the extra 1% be seen as being justified? Of course! However, if you paid the 1% extra and underperformed the market, you'd be pretty upset and rightly so. That's why knowing how to pick the right fund is crucial.

The choice of whether you opt for active or passive will depend on your situation and many factors will have to be considered. For me personally, it makes sense to mainly go with actively managed funds. Sometimes I may buy a tracker fund but most of the time I stick to actively managed funds and I don't mind paying a little bit extra for them.

However, as you'll see in **Chapter 11: Creating an Income for Life**, for capital outside an ISA and SIPP, there is a 'passive' strategy that could help you reap annual returns of 7–10% over the long term. The reason I prefer actively managed over passive for my ISA and SIPP accounts is because I know from experience that it's possible, after all investment and advisory fees and charges have been taken into consideration, to outperform the market and therefore beat tracker funds.

This means that with active investing, if you know what you are doing, you can achieve a better return than the general market. It's not easy, but possible. Of course, I don't outperform the market every year, but I am proud that I've outperformed it over the last 16 years and that's after all the costs of investing have been taken into consideration[32]. My take is, what happens on the journey in the short term is simply commentary as long as you end up at your chosen long-term destination.

My friend, I am pleased to inform you that we've got the 'beginner' content out of the way, which means we can now move on to the more sophisticated material. This is information that many of our clients call 'the secret sauce.'

Let me ask you a question.

Would you be interested in learning my unique strategy for choosing funds that perform?

What about discovering how I find funds that are 'in the money flow' and exhibit superior sustainable growth potential?

You would?

That's great, because next you are going to learn my complete strategy for picking winning funds. I'm also going to introduce you to my 7 tips for fund picking success and 'The Performance Quadrant' – a tool I developed to help determine your future expected return. You're also going to discover HIRE CAR™, a fund screening tool I created that provides expert guidance when looking for quality investment funds. Let's go and find out…

6: How to Pick a Good Fund

'We rate fund managers rather than funds. We believe the most important factor in investment decisions is how good the fund manager is.'
– Citywire.co.uk

When investing for growth, many people seek out funds suited to more adventurous investors. These types of funds are volatile in the short term but, if you hold them over the long term and choose well, they can help you reap impressive returns.

The objective of these types of funds is long-term capital growth however, be aware that they are not for the faint hearted. This type of investing is aimed at investors who have at least 5 years as their investment horizon, but preferably 10.

7 Tips for Fund Picking Success

Before we look at the steps I personally take to find a good fund, I'd like to share my 7 tips for fund picking success. By understanding the big picture it will give you a good overview of the way I think about investing in funds, my investment philosophy and my investment strategy.

Tip 1 – Market Trend and Direction

I only invest in equity based funds when I believe the market is in a confirmed uptrend (bull market). When I believe a major downtrend (bear market) has been triggered I switch out of an equities based fund into a Cash Park to protect potential downside losses. If you have a SIPP, you can park in cash using a SIPP Bank Account. The last time I moved into cash was during the last bear market of 2007–2009.

The reason I move out of higher risk investments and into low risk ones is because my aim is to get in sync with the stock market's trend and direction. This is because institutional investors account for approximately 75% of the market's movement, which means it's important to follow their lead. When you don't get in sync, it feels like trying to run against a strong headwind. You'll learn how to read the markets trend and direction in **Chapter 8: Gauging Stock Market Direction**.

Tip 2 – Tax-Efficient Investing

One way I've found to help you beat the market and boost your returns is to wrap an ISA and a SIPP around the investment funds you buy. And remember that any pension contributions you decide to make will get a boost from the Government.

By using tax wrappers, all of the gains you make will be protected from the taxman. This means you have no capital gains tax (CGT) to pay on the profits you make when you move in and out of the market. You see, when you invest in funds outside an ISA or SIPP, you have to pay CGT and this alone can seriously hurt your total returns for the year. Beating the market without the use of a tax wrapper makes the task at hand much more difficult.

Tip 3 – Long-Term Past Performance

Investment performance is the most important element in fund selection. I look at the fund's long-term performance results to see if the fund has been outperforming the NASDAQ Composite in bull market periods.

Tip 4 – The Fund's Present Manager

I always check to see how long the present manager of the fund has been managing it. I look for the date the manager started because it's important to ensure that the current fund manager is the one who has scored the impressive past performance results.

Tip 5 – Short-Term Past Performance

My aim is to locate and lock in on fund managers who are in the middle of the money flow. To do this, I look for funds that are performing well in the short term.

Tip 6 – Fund Chart

Charts help me time my buys and exits. When I'm buying, I look for bullish chart patterns, such as cup-with-handles and double bottoms. From a safety point of view, and to make sure I buy at the optimum time, I aim to buy when the fund breaks out of a sound base. I'll be showing you how to time your buys and exits in the next chapter.

Tip 7 – Fight for Every Percentage Point

It's possible to keep fees, commissions and trading costs low by buying your fund using a fund supermarket. As you've already discovered, if you don't go through a fund supermarket you could pay as much as 5.5% in upfront fees.

You are likely to need at least some growth

Inflation runs at around 3% per year and annual charges for actively managed funds can be in the region of 1–3%. That means you've got to make 4–6% per year just to ensure your wealth is not stuck in reverse gear. Therefore, if you have a life expectancy of 20 years or more, you are likely to need at least some growth and the most effective way of achieving that growth is to invest in equities. This can be done by buying equity based investment funds.

Capital market returns for the United Kingdom

The chart shows that over the last 111 years, the real value of equities with income reinvested, grew by a factor of 317 as compared to 4.6 for bonds and 3.1 for bills.

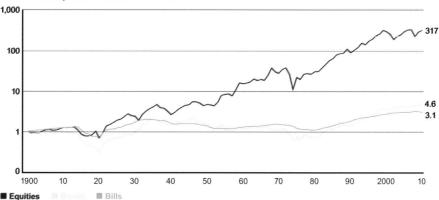

Annualised performance from 1900 to 2010

■ **Equities**   ■ Bonds   ■ Bills

Source: Credit Suisse

A key thing to remember is that, when seeking long-term growth and higher returns for your ISA and SIPP, your main objective should be to beat the market.

What exactly does the term, 'beat the market' mean?

There are many names and phrases to describe beating the market, such as outperforming the market, beating the indexes and staying ahead of the indices, but they all mean the same thing, which is doing better than a particular benchmark. Where people's opinions do differ is when it comes to the benchmark they measure their performance against.

In other words, which market, index, or indices are they trying to beat? Our aim is to help our clients beat the NASDAQ Composite. The NASDAQ Composite, the main US technology index, is one of the strongest market indexes in the world in terms of price performance. Over the long term, the NASDAQ has made an average yearly gain of 18.3%[33].

And so, with the NASDAQ being such a powerful index, it means it's a difficult task to beat it. Take a look at this chart illustration (page 85) displaying how the NASDAQ Composite has performed versus the FTSE 100. As you can see, since 1984, the FTSE 100 made just over 400%. However, the NASDAQ is the clear winner after making more than 1000% over the very same period.

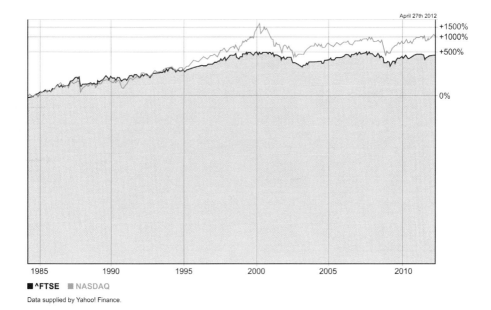

April 27th 2012

■ ^FTSE ■ NASDAQ

Data supplied by Yahoo! Finance.

Aiming to beat the NASDAQ would therefore be a much tougher goal than trying to beat the FTSE 100, but it is a worthy goal for adventurous long-term investors who seek attractive returns. Outperforming the NASDAQ Composite over the long term is an extremely tough task.

However, beating it could be your objective if your goal, like mine, is to achieve market beating returns. Beating the market is important because it helps you achieve higher returns, allowing you to arrive at your financial goals faster. Failing to beat the market means it takes you longer to reach your goals and in some cases, you never reach them at all.

The Performance Quadrant

It's important to know that, when investing for growth, the size of your annual returns will always depend on four factors. The

Performance Quadrant was a model I created to highlight these four factors and it's based on the notion that when investing in the stock market, there are some things that are in your control and some things that aren't. The Performance Quadrant is made up of four parts, with two of the components being in your control and two being out of your control.

As there are two components that are out of your control, it's unfortunately impossible to predict the exact size of the returns you are likely to make. However, as you will soon see, because you do have two elements within your control, if you handle those two parts well, it could increase your chances of achieving better returns over the long term.

The Performance Quadrant

Internal (in your control)   External (out of your control)

Investment Vehicle   Market Direction

Market Timing   Market Strength

Courtesy of ISACO.co.uk.

Investment Vehicle

The first part of the quadrant is the Investment Vehicle and, in this example, we are going to use a favourite of mine; funds. It's common sense that if you choose well, it will have a positive effect on your investment returns and if you choose badly, it will have a negative effect. But what should your buying criteria be?

If you are an adventurous investor like me, with a long-term time horizon, your aim would be to choose high quality investment funds – funds that have the greatest potential for swift price rises from the moment they are purchased. This is a difficult task but made easier with knowledge and lots of practice. Your objective would be to buy 'best of breed' funds that exhibit superior sustainable growth potential and hold them for as long as they demonstrate outperformance.

Market Timing

The second part of The Performance Quadrant is Market Timing. The timing of your buys and exits are also in your control. Because three out of every four funds move in the same direction as the general market, my suggestion would be to try to invest in bull markets and aim to stay on the sidelines in bear markets.

When a major downtrend is triggered (bear market), the objective is to switch out of equity funds and into cash to preserve your wealth. This sounds easy in theory, however it's very difficult in practice. Market timing is made easier by daily studying of the price and volume activity of institutional investors. We'll look at this in great depth in the next chapter and in **Chapter 8: Gauging Stock Market Direction**.

Market Direction

The third part of The Performance Quadrant is Market Direction. Market direction is out of your control as it's impossible to 'will' the market up. And if the market does not go up, funds are not going to go up either. The annual returns of the funds you choose throughout your investing career will be directly linked to the market's direction. If the market is trending up, three out of every four funds will move up. If the market is trending downwards, funds are going to move down. And if the market is trending sideways, they are going to move sideways.

Market Strength

The fourth and final part of The Performance Quadrant is Market Strength. The strength of the market's trend is also out of your control. If the market is trending up and the trend is strong, fund performance will be impressive. For example, in 1999, the NASDAQ Composite gained 86% in one year! During that year, investment funds were moving up 100%, 200%, 300% and even 400% – over a 12 month period. The rule is: quality investment funds make substantial gains when the market is strong.

Hopefully, you will now be able to see the link between the funds you buy, the market's direction, the market's strength and the investment returns you achieve. With this in mind, I suggest you set different aims for different market environments. For example, our aims are based on a period of 5–15 years.

1) Sideways trending market: our aim is 3–5% per annum

2) Upwards trending market: our aim is 8–10% per annum
3) Very strong upwards trending market: our aim is 12–15% per annum

A different slant on past performance

Private investors are constantly reminded that past performance is no indication of what will happen in the future. However, when you view past performance in a different light, it can help give you an edge when choosing the best funds to buy. When choosing the best fund manager to park your money with, it's best to think in probabilities rather than certainties.

Nothing is guaranteed when investing in the stock market, which means you need to do all you can to increase the probability that the fund manager you choose will continue to perform well in the future. When seeking a good return on your ISA and SIPP over the long term, my suggestion would be to aim to find fund managers with outstanding track records.

The way this works is pretty simple: when the market is in a confirmed uptrend, I scan for funds managed by exceptional fund managers. I like to ensure that the fund manager has proven they can beat the market in the short and the long term.

The fund managers I like to focus on

If you followed a similar strategy to mine, your aim would be to make sure the person managing the fund has outperformed the market in the long term, and in the short term. You simply compare the manager's performance versus a benchmark, such as the FTSE 100, the S&P 500 or the NASDAQ Composite.

As you've discovered, the majority of fund managers underperform the market, however a small percentage do actually beat it and these are the fund managers I like to focus on. The NASDAQ is a tough index to beat and when I find exceptional fund managers, I often notice that they not only beat the NASDAQ in one year, they beat it in multiple years and this means their beating the market was not achieved by luck.

As well as looking at how these fund managers have performed year on year (long term), I like to make sure that the fund manager has proven they can outperform the market in the short term. The short-term analysis allows me to see which managers are really in sync with the market. The best ones will be the ones who are holding the market's leading stocks and, when I look at their recent short-term performance, I usually see that they have easily been beating the NASDAQ.

Priceless information

Some fund managers with great track records will unfortunately not be in sync with the market and not in the money flow. Why? Each fund manager has an objective and a mandate that they have to stick to, such as only investing in Japanese stocks, British stocks or possibly American stocks. Some managers' mandates state that they can only invest in a particular sector, such as the technology sector or the basic resources sector. The important thing to understand here is that all fund managers have a brief and they have to stick to it.

This puts many top fund managers at a disadvantage because the big money can only flow into a handful of countries/sectors, rather than flowing into every country in the world and every given sector. This is one of the reasons why most top managers are never going to be able to constantly outperform the market every single year.

That's why I follow the mantra of aiming to invest in exceptional fund managers – managers who hold stocks where the big money is flowing right now. These are the fund managers I class as being in sync with the market. These are funds controlled by fund managers who have not only proved they can beat the NASDAQ in the long term; they are also beating the NASDAQ in the short term.

HIRE CAR™

HIRE CAR™ is a screening tool I created to help me quickly find quality investment funds. HIRE CAR™ is an acronym, which means that each letter in HIRE CAR™ relates to a particular part of the formula, these being:

H = Health
I = ISA
R = Results
E = Exceptional Performance

C = Count Stars and Chart Pattern
A = Anywhere in the World
R = Recent Performance

HIRE CAR™ explained

The HIRE CAR™ formula is made of these key components:

H = Health

I only invest in quality investment funds when I believe the market is in a confirmed uptrend (bull market). When I believe the market is a confirmed downtrend (bear market), I park in cash to protect potential downside losses.

I = ISA

The funds I choose must allow me to invest through my ISAs and SIPP. This means all of the gains I make will be protected from the taxman and I will never have any capital gains tax to pay on my profits when I move in and out of the market – helping to increase my investment returns.

R = Results

Performance is the most important element in fund selection and that means I like to discover who the fund manager is and I look at the fund manager's long-term performance results. I check to see if the manager has been managing the fund over the previous bull market period. I look for the date the current fund manager started managing the fund because it's important to ensure the current fund manager is the manager who has scored the impressive results.

E = Exceptional Performance

Ideally, I want to see the fund manager outperforming the NASDAQ Composite in bull market periods. To achieve this objective I look at how the NASDAQ performed in previous bull market periods.

NASDAQ Composite performance in bull markets							
2003	2004	2005	2006	2007	2009	2010	2012
50%	8.6%	1.4%	9.5%	9.8%	43.9%	16.9%	15.9%

Courtesy of ISACO.co.uk.

I generally ignore how the manager performed in the down years (the bear market years) but if they beat the market in those years too, it's a bonus.

NASDAQ Composite performance in bear markets				
2000	2001	2002	2008	2011
-39.3%	-21.1%	-31.5%	-40.5%	-1.8%

Courtesy of ISACO.co.uk.

C = Count & Chart

Quality investment funds normally have four or five Morningstar stars and we'll be looking at Morningstar in greater depth in a moment. If a fund has three stars or fewer, I only give it a stamp of approval if the fund manager's performance is exceptional.

Some funds I've bought have only had one star and they've turned out to be big winners, which is a lesson in never relying solely on a star rating system. When it comes to the fund's chart, I look for bullish chart patterns such as cup-with-handles, flat bases, saucers-with-handles and double bottoms. It is best to purchase funds as they break out of a sound base. You'll learn more about timing your buys and exits in the next chapter.

A = Anywhere in the World

My guidelines state that the investment fund can invest anywhere in the world but I prefer it if the country the fund invests in has a strong and stable economy. The US, Japanese, Chinese, UK and most European funds are always worth exploring, as long as the fund manager's performance is excellent. I like to invest in a fund that is diversified but if I find a fund that has a specialty in say one or two sectors, I ensure that they are sectors likely to lead in bull markets, such as internet, semiconductors, medical, telecom, retail, computer, metals or energy.

R = Recent Performance

When the market is healthy, and it's clearly in an uptrend, one of the things I scan for is how funds are performing in the short term. This short-term period action could be the previous day, week, month and possibly even the previous quarter. This is just as important as looking at the fund manager's longer term performance.

Funds with outstanding growth potential

The website that I like to use when searching for the best funds is Morningstar. You can find it by going to www.morningstar.co.uk. Before you invest, I suggest you aim to find out if we are in a bull market or a bear market and one way you can do this is by looking at an index chart. Which index or indexes you choose to look at to help you track the market is your own decision. However, my favourite, as you've heard, is the NASDAQ Composite.

Bull market or bear market? Where are we?

For the purpose of this exercise, it's important for you to be aware that I took the up and coming screenshots on August 27th 2013. As you can see on this 20 year chart of the NASDAQ Composite, the present bull market started back in March 2009 (Point A) and since then, it's clearly formed a strong uptrend (Point B).

Charts are copyright © 2013 MarketSmith, Incorporated. All rights reserved.
Unauthorized duplication, modification, photocopying or distribution in any form is strictly prohibited. Reprinted with permission.

Keep this in mind, because when we do our searches on Morningstar we'll be looking at which funds have performed best over the last five years. I say five years because when I took these screenshots, the bull market had been running for just under four and a half years.

On this 12 month chart of the NASDAQ Composite, there is a clear uptrend. The uptrend starts November 16th 2012 (Point C) and is currently nine months old (Point D).

The facts so far about the market:
- The market had been in an uptrend for just under four and a half years.
- The market had been in an uptrend over the last nine months.

Just before we move on, I want you to make a mental note: The gain made by the NASDAQ over the previous nine months was 30.1%. We'll be using this as a benchmark later so that we can measure the nine month gain against the fund's performance over this same period.

Morningstar home page

This is Morningstar's home page. To start our search we click on the 'ISA' tab. We do this because it's not possible to purchase some funds within a stocks and shares ISA. We therefore want to make sure that when we conduct our searches, all the funds we'll be looking at are 'ISA friendly'.

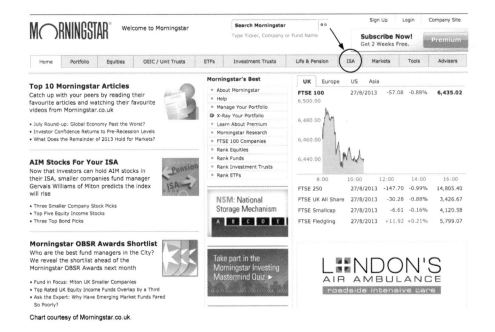

Chart courtesy of Morningstar.co.uk.

ISA Funds to Explore

As you discovered earlier, the market had been in a bull market for almost five years and so next, where it says 'ISA Funds To Explore', we are going to look at the ISA funds that have performed the best over the last 5 years. We can do that by clicking on the tab that says '5 Year Returns'.

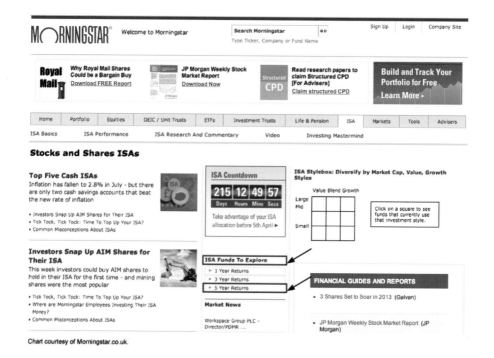

Chart courtesy of Morningstar.co.uk.

5 Year Performance

On this next image (page 99), you see the highest ranking funds in terms of 5 year performance. We could look at any of these funds on this list however we are going to view one that I know well. It's called the Cazenove UK Smaller Companies A Acc. Let's click on its link to take a closer look.

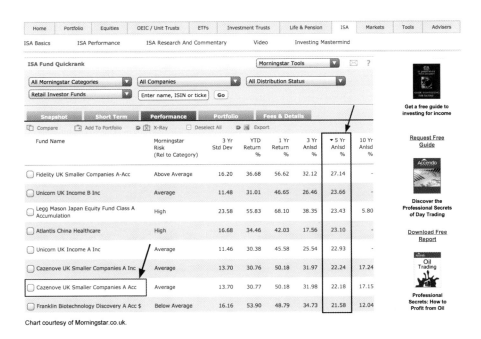

Chart courtesy of Morningstar.co.uk.

Overview Page

Here you can see what Morningstar call the 'Overview' page of the fund.

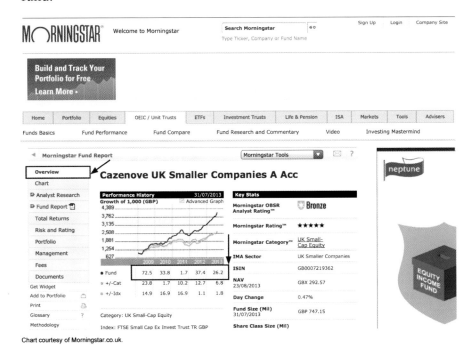

Chart courtesy of Morningstar.co.uk.

The first thing I focus on when searching for a fund, which I believe to be the most important part of fund selection, is the fund's past performance. I start off by looking at how it has performed since the bull market began. As you can see, it returned 72.5% in 2009, 33.8% in 2010, 1.8% in 2011, 37.4% in 2012 and, year to date in 2013, it had made a gain of 26.2%.

When you punch those annual return figures into a calculator, you discover that the fund had made a total return of 307%. This is what you'd class as extremely impressive performance. The NASDAQ Composite over the same period had made a return of 43.9% in 2009, 16.9% in 2010, -5.6% in 2011, 15.9% in 2012 and, when this screenshot was taken, it had made a year to date return of 21.1%.

That gives the NASDAQ a total return of 122.9% over the same period. This comparison of total returns between the fund and the NASDAQ Composite tells us that over the four and a half year bull market period, the Cazenove UK Smaller Companies A Acc fund had easily beaten one of the world's strongest indexes – so far so good.

When did the current manager start managing this fund?

Managers of funds can get sacked or they might leave on their own accord. Fund managers therefore move around and that's why you have to get the direct connection between the fund's performance and the manager who is *currently* managing the fund. With this in mind, let's look at who is currently managing this fund by clicking on the 'Management' tab located in the left hand column.

Chart courtesy of Morningstar.co.uk.

Management

On this page we discover that the fund manager, Paul Marriage started managing this fund on January 3rd 2006. Therefore, the performance we looked at before is his. This also means that we are now safe to continue with our analysis. Next, we'll look at the fund's risk rating by clicking on the 'Risk and Rating' tab located in the left hand column.

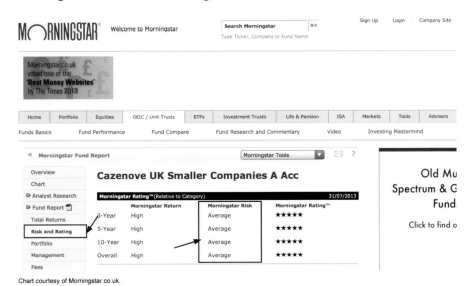

Chart courtesy of Morningstar.co.uk.

Risk and Rating

What we find here is that this fund's risk profile is average. Almost all the funds I buy are classed average or above average risk. If you are aiming for growth, the fund you'll need to choose is likely to be in a higher risk category and I see this as perfectly normal. Next, we'll look at the fund's portfolio to get a breakdown of its current holdings.

At the top of this page, you get to see the manager's investment style. This fund invests in small companies but generally I prefer to see the manager investing in giant, large cap or medium cap stocks. This is because in my opinion larger companies carry less risk and have less chance of going bust in the future.

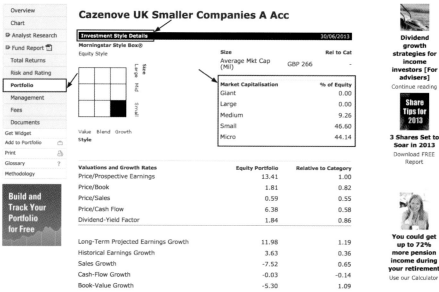

Chart courtesy of Morningstar.co.uk.

Portfolio

If we stay on the Portfolio tab, underneath the 'Investment Style Details' you can see the fund's 'Asset Allocation' and 'World Regions'.

Asset Allocation			30/06/2013
	% Long	% Short	% Net Assets
Stock	95.86	0.00	95.86
Bond	0.00	0.00	0.00
Property	0.00	0.00	0.00
Cash	5.99	2.05	3.93
Other	0.20	0.00	0.20

World Regions		30/06/2013
	% of Equity	Relative to Category
United States	0.00	0.00
Canada	1.55	2.31
Latin America	0.00	0.00
United Kingdom	97.33	1.02
Eurozone	1.12	0.62
Europe - ex Euro	0.00	0.00
Europe - Emerging	0.00	0.00
Africa	0.00	0.00
Middle East	0.00	0.00
Japan	0.00	-
Australasia	0.00	0.00
Asia - Developed	0.00	0.00
Asia - Emerging	0.00	0.00

Chart courtesy of Morningstar.co.uk.

In the funds that we buy, their asset allocation is usually 95 to 100% invested 'Long' in stock. Sometimes they hold a bit of cash and I'm fine with that. With the 'World Region' details, it simply tells you what part of the world the fund is investing in and with this fund you can see that it's the United Kingdom.

Asset Allocation

Scroll down the Portfolio page a little further and you'll see the sector weightings.

Sector Weightings	30/06/2013	
	% of Equity	Relative to Category
Basic Materials	2.72	0.51
Consumer Cyclical	23.29	1.07
Financial Services	7.53	0.76
Real Estate	7.96	1.34
Consumer Defensive	8.53	2.05
Healthcare	4.84	0.85
Utilities	0.58	1.61
Communication Services	2.86	1.07
Energy	0.16	0.03
Industrials	19.88	0.82
Technology	21.65	1.42

Chart courtesy of Morningstar.co.uk.

I like to see that the fund is diversified into many different sectors which means this one passes the criteria. If the fund was too heavily weighted in one sector, it may cause me to reject it. Scroll down to the bottom of the Portfolio tab and you'll see the number of stocks in the fund, the percentage of assets in the top 10 holdings and also the names of the stocks that make up the fund's top 10 holdings.

Top 10 Holdings			30/06/2013
			Portfolio
Total Number of Equity Holdings			74
Total Number of Bond Holdings			0
Assets in Top 10 Holdings			25.72
Name	Sector	Country	% of Assets
Xaar PLC		United Kingdom	3.92
Perform Group PLC		United Kingdom	3.32
Menzies (John) PLC		United Kingdom	3.12
Cranswick PLC		United Kingdom	2.76
Esure Group PLC		United Kingdom	2.51
Hansteen Holdings PLC		United Kingdom	2.20
Telford Homes PLC		United Kingdom	2.01
Smart Metering Systems PLC		United Kingdom	1.99
Clinigen Group PLC		United Kingdom	1.94
Pendragon PLC		United Kingdom	1.94

Chart courtesy of Morningstar.co.uk.

By knowing what stocks the fund holds, it allows me to carry out further due diligence and check if the stocks the fund holds are classed as leaders. I do this by using an equity research package called MarketSmith (more about MarketSmith in **Chapter 10: How to Manage Your Portfolio**).

Chart

Next, we'll look at the fund's chart. But first I want to take you back and remind you what the market had done recently. If you remember, when the image was taken the return made over the previous nine months was 30.1%. We can use that return as a performance benchmark to measure against.

1 year view

When you click on the Chart tab in the left hand column, the default chart shown is a 1 year view of the fund's performance. To get an unobstructed view of its performance, you need to click on the three 'X's' that show FTSE Small Cap Ex Investment Tru…, UK Small-Cap Equity and UK Smaller Companies.

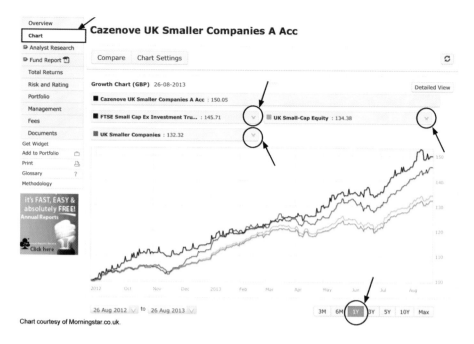

YTD chart view

Next, click on the 'Chart Settings' tab.

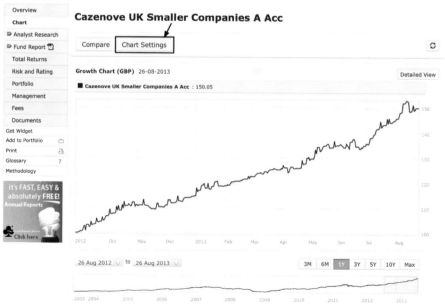

Now click on 'Display Options'.

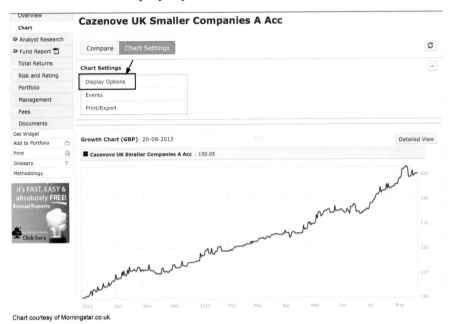

Chart courtesy of Morningstar.co.uk.

To view the fund's price, click on the 'Percentage' tab. Notice the price scale that appears on the right hand side of the chart.

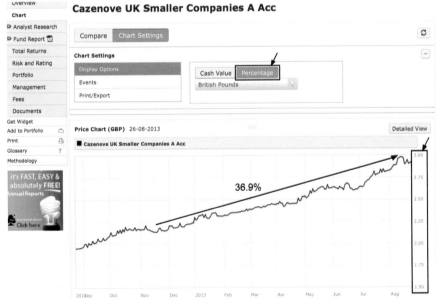

Chart courtesy of Morningstar.co.uk.

Past prices

To check how the fund has performed over any period, you simply hover your mouse pointer over the image, allowing you to see past prices of the fund. When I hovered over this one to locate November 16th 2012 (the date the NASDAQ Composite started its nine month uptrend), I found out that the fund was trading at 2.14 and on August 27th 2013, when this screenshot was taken, it was trading at 2.93, a 36.9% nine month return.

With the NASDAQ Composite making a 30.1% return over the same period, it provided evidence that this fund was outperforming the NASDAQ in the short term as well as the long term – and that's exactly what I'm looking for. Next, we'll look at the fund's fees and charges.

Fees and Expenses

The 'Fees and Expenses' section is split into two areas: Sales Charges (Maximum) and Annual Charges.

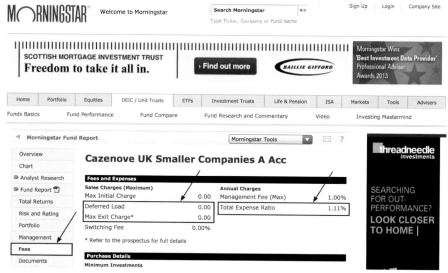

Chart courtesy of Morningstar.co.uk.

The Deferred Load (a charge taken when you sell) shows a 0 and so does the Max Exit Charge which is ideally what I like to see. The total expense ratio (TER) is 1.11% which is fairly low and this is because this fund has a clean share class. It's always good practice to double check this figure versus what it says on the fund's Key Investor Information Document (KIID). You can find the KIID and other associated documents in the 'Documents' section. We'll look at the Documents tab next.

Documents

The one I always look at first is the Key Investor Information Document (KIID). To view the KIID, you click on the small PDF icon in the KIID row.

Chart courtesy of Morningstar.co.uk.

This is a two page document which means you can quickly get to the information that's important. On page one you can check the risk profile of the fund. The ones I purchase usually score 6 or 7 on a scale of 1 to 7. As you can see, this one scores a 6.

CAZENOVE
CAPITAL MANAGEMENT

Key Investor Information

This document provides you with key investor information about this fund. It is not marketing material. The information is required by law to help you understand the nature and the risks of investing in this fund. You are advised to read it so you can make an informed decision about whether to invest.

Cazenove UK Smaller Companies Fund
A Class Accumulation

A sub-fund of Cazenove Investment Fund Company (CIFCO)

This fund is managed by Cazenove Investment Fund Management Limited (CIFM)

ISIN: GB0007219362

SEDOL: 0721936

Objectives and Investment Policy

- The fund seeks to achieve long term capital growth.
- The fund buys high quality UK listed smaller companies capable of producing above average growth in earnings and dividends over the medium to long term.
- The fund has a broadly spread portfolio that reduces the specific investment risks of smaller companies.
- You can buy and sell shares in the fund on demand on any day on which the London Stock Exchange is open for business.

- The fund's benchmark is the FTSE SmallCap (ex IT) Index.
- The fund selects its own investments.
- The fund may not be appropriate if you plan to withdraw your money within 5 years.
- The shares are accumulation shares. This means that any income received into the fund from its investments is retained within the fund on its distribution date rather than being paid out. This retained income is reflected in the share price. There are two distribution date(s) each year.

Risk and Reward Profile

Lower risk						Higher risk
Potentially lower reward						Potentially higher reward
1	2	3	4	5	**6**	7

The risk indicator for this fund is 6 because:
- The fund invests in small companies which may be risky and may be difficult to sell with the result that the fund's share price may fluctuate more markedly than a fund that invests in larger companies.
- Investment in shares and/or bonds is subject to normal market fluctuations. There is no assurance that your investment will increase in value. Your original investment is not guaranteed.
- The value of the fund may fluctuate significantly in response to the performance of individual companies, as well as in connection with market and economic conditions.
- The fund's risk profile is based on historical data and this may not be a reliable indicator of its future risk profile.

- The lowest risk category does not mean an investment is risk free.
- The risk category shown is not a target or a guarantee and may change over time.

Other relevant risks:
- Operational risk: The risk that there is a significant loss to the fund from human error, systems failure, inadequate controls or internal management mistakes.
- Settlement risk: The risk of loss if there is late or non payment for the assets sold by the fund.
- Liquidity risk: The risk that it is hard for the fund to buy or sell shares for its portfolio because of a reduction of buying and selling activity in stock markets.
- Valuation risk: The risk that an asset held by the fund is mispriced.

Further details on risk are set out in the Prospectus in the section Risk Factors.

Next we are going to look at page two of the KIID and cross-check its TER or 'ongoing charges' with the TER you saw on the 'Fees and Expenses' page. It should be the same and as you can see on this image, we have a match.

Charges

The charges you pay contribute to the costs of running the fund, including the cost of distributing it, reducing the potential growth of your investment.

One-off charges taken before or after you invest	
Entry charge	0.00%
Exit charge	0.00%

Charges taken from the fund over a year	
Ongoing charges	1.11%

Charges taken from the fund under certain specific conditions	
Performance fee	none

You can find out the actual entry and exit charge from your financial adviser or distributor.

The ongoing charge is taken from the fund's income rather than its investments.

The ongoing charge figure is based on last year's expenses, year-ending December 2012. This figure may vary from year to year. It excludes the cost of buying and selling investments held by the fund.

For more information on charges please see the Charges & Expenses section of the Prospectus.

Past Performance

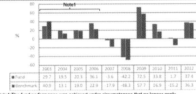

Note1: The fund performance was achieved under circumstances that no longer apply.

Past performance is calculated in GBP.

Past performance is not indicative of future performance. It cannot provide a guarantee of returns that you will receive in the future.

The value of your investment and income from it may go down as well as up and you may not get back the amount you invested. All fees and charges are included in the performance calculation.

The fund was launched on 06 May 1999 and issued A Class Accumulation shares on 06 May 1999.

Practical Information

CIFCO is an umbrella structure comprising this and other sub-funds. The fund's current share price is calculated on each Business Day and is published daily on our website. The depositary of the fund is J.P. Morgan Trustee and Depositary Company Limited.

You may switch between this fund's share classes and other sub-funds of CIFCO as long as you meet the appropriate requirements.

The tax legislation of the fund's home Member State and of your country of residence may impact on the buying and selling of shares and any distributions paid by the fund. Taxation is subject to change. You should consult your professional adviser if you have any questions.

The assets and liabilities of each sub-fund are segregated by law therefore a sub-fund will not be liable for the debts of another sub-fund if the assets are insufficient to meet its liabilities.

CIFM may be held liable solely on the basis of any statement contained in this document that is misleading, inaccurate or inconsistent with the relevant parts of the Prospectus.

This Key Investor Information document (KIId) is specific to this share class. KIIds are available for other share classes within this fund. However, the Prospectus and annual and half-yearly Report and Accounts are prepared to cover all sub-funds of CIFCO.

Further information about the fund including other share classes, switching and dealing can be found in the Prospectus, available in English, and also in the latest annual and half-yearly Report and Accounts (English only) which are available free of charge by calling +44 (0)20 3479 0000 or can be downloaded from the Literature Library section of our website www.cazenovecapital.com.

This fund is authorised in the United Kingdom and regulated by the Financial Services Authority. Cazenove Investment Fund Management Limited is authorised in the United Kingdom and regulated by the Financial Services Authority. This key investor information is accurate as at 31/01/2013.

You can find other key documents relating to funds on the trading platform or fund supermarket that you decide to use. As well as looking at the Key Investor Information Document (KIID), I pay close attention to the Fund FactSheet, the Associated Charges Document, Client Terms, plus other associated documents such as the Shareholders' documents, which include the Interim Short Report and the Annual Short Report.

This exercise was designed to show you what I look for when seeking a good fund, and carried out for illustrative purposes only. Hopefully, by taking you through it step by step, it will have helped you understand more about my strategy and investment philosophy when selecting funds to buy.

I'm sure that you're pretty excited about what you've just learned and can't wait to start having a play on the Morningstar website. But you may be thinking, *'Okay, I now know how to pick a good fund but I'm still unsure exactly when I should be buying it, whether to hold onto it, and when to sell it for a profit.'*

If you are thinking along those lines, I have some good news. Next we are going to look in great detail at how to time your buys and exits. This is the main thing that prospective clients want help with when they contact us. If that rings true with you too, you are going to find this next chapter extremely valuable.

You'll find out how to buy a fund at the optimum time and why it's key to recognise two specific trading patterns and determine ideal buy points. You'll also discover the three things I use to help me decide when to sell a fund and why I don't always use stop losses.

Would that be useful?

Great, because you are about to find out all you need to know about…

7: Fund Timing: When to Buy and When to Exit

'Major advances occur off strong, recognizable price patterns.'
– William O'Neil

After speaking to a huge number of DIY investors over the past 16 years, we've learned that many feel reasonably comfortable selecting which funds to invest in but have problems knowing when to buy and when to exit. We've also found that most investors become uncertain about whether to hold on to their fund once they've bought it, especially if it drops in price just after they've purchased it.

They also tend to get very nervous as soon as it experiences its first major correction – which of course all funds will do. They think, *is this normal? Should I sell it or should I hold? What if I sell it and it goes up? What if I keep it and it continues to go lower?* You see, when a fund heads south, many private investors have no idea whether the behaviour is normal and healthy or abnormal and unhealthy.

Timing the market is not easy

Because of this lack of financial literacy, the uneducated investor will make a decision based on how they feel, which in most cases will unfortunately turn out to be a bad call. The thing is, getting your timing right is very difficult and requires knowledge, skill and tons of experience. I do this for a living and I never get my timing right all the time.

To become good, it takes lots of effort and bags of patience. If it's really important to you to become good in timing the market, I'm certain that the guidelines presented in this chapter will help you to eventually master it. And if you do become good at it, this newly acquired skill of yours will probably result in a marked improvement in your investment returns.

Let's start by looking at when to buy.

When to buy

Buying a fund at the optimum time starts with looking at the current market direction. Why? The majority of stocks (approximately 75%) tend to move in the same direction as the market. Funds own stocks and therefore funds also move in the same direction as the market. Therefore, even if you are fantastic at picking the best fund, if you are wrong about the trend of the market your portfolio is going to suffer.

Markets work in cycles and consist of a bull and a bear market. Bull markets are the upwards part of the cycle and last between two and four years. Bear markets head downwards and last approximately nine to eighteen months. Because bull markets last longer, the stock market over the long term forms an uptrend. Think of a staircase and think three stairs up (bull market), one stair down (bear market). In the next chapter, you'll learn everything you need to know about reading the market's health, trend and likely future direction.

Find a fund that's suitable

Once you've completed your analysis of the market, if you believe that it's in a long-term uptrend (bull market), your focus can then move towards finding a fund that matches your risk profile and objectives. As you now know, I like to focus on the past performance of the present fund manager and I also like to make sure that the manager has proved that they have beaten the market in the past and are beating it right now.

Check its chart pattern

Once you're happy with market direction and you've identified a fund that you like and you feel is suitable, the last part of the jigsaw is timing your buy. The key is being able to recognise two specific trading patterns as well as determining the proper buy points. Before a fund can launch a big price run up, it must have a solid base pattern to build upon. Base patterns occur when a fund's price falls and consolidates over a series of weeks or months or even years.

Most of them (80–90%) are created and formed as a result of corrections in the general market. Bases typically form after a fund has already experienced a nice increase in its price – also known as an uptrend – of at least 30%. That uptrend is important because it shows you the fund has built up a record of price growth already, and the stocks the fund owns have received support from some big professional investors. There are several kinds of bases that winning funds frequently form prior to a big price run-up.

Let's look at the two most popular:

Cup-with-handle base pattern

Learning to recognise the cup-with-handle pattern on a chart helps you aim to buy in before the fund begins its big run. The cup-with-handle base is one of the easiest patterns to spot – and probably the most powerful. On a chart it resembles a teacup as seen from its side view.

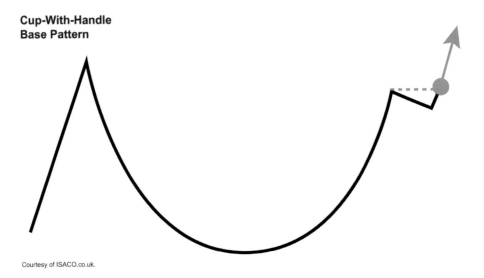

Cup-With-Handle Base Pattern

Courtesy of ISACO.co.uk.

During the final stage of the base – after the fund has climbed up the right side of the pattern – it may pull back, etching a downward-sloping handle on its chart. The key is to watch for the fund price 'breaking out' of the pattern, which is the best time to buy.

Three cup-with-handle examples

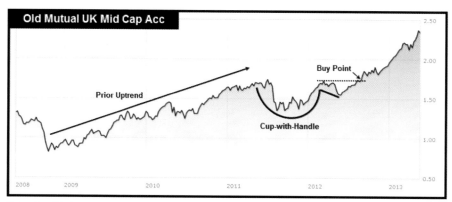

Chart courtesy of Morningstar.co.uk.

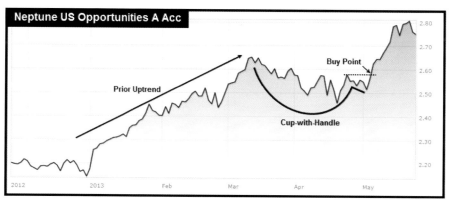

Chart courtesy of Morningstar.co.uk

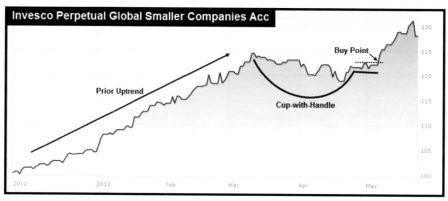

Chart courtesy of Morningstar.co.uk.

Buying at the wrong time

Some investors who learn about cup-with-handle formations ask the question, 'why not buy when the fund is at the bottom of its base at a lower price?' The reason we avoid buying at the bottom is simply because it's too risky. From our experience, we've found that buying at the bottom of the base results in a greater likelihood that the fund will head either lower or sideways (instead of upwards) after purchasing it.

Buying too early

Next, I want to show you two examples of funds we personally owned where we bought too early. The first is the Fidelity Funds – India Focus Fund A-GBP.

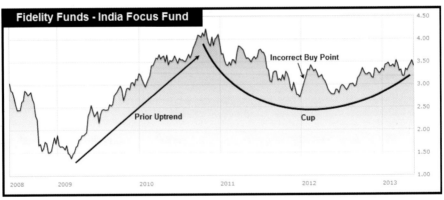

Chart courtesy of Morningstar.co.uk.

We bought this one on January 24th 2012 at a price of 3.12 and sold it on March 11th 2013 at 3.53. Even though we made a 13.1% gain in 14 months, we sold it because when we buy a fund our expectations are for it to outperform the market however, this one underperformed.

The second example of a fund we bought too early is one called the Neptune Russia & Greater Russia A. We bought and sold this fund on exactly the same days that we bought and sold the India fund.

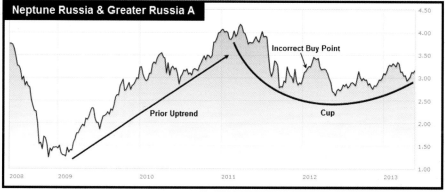

Chart courtesy of Morningstar.co.uk.

This one performed even worse than the India fund and resulted in a 1.6% loss. A loss of less than 2% might not seem that bad but during the period we held it, the market was moving up and so were many funds. These two mistakes were sloppy of me. I very rarely deviate from my rule of aiming to buy funds when they are breaking out into new high ground however, after making the fatal mistake of trying to get in early, it reminded me that trying to buy low is a flawed strategy.

I've found that it's always best to buy when the fund has plenty of upwards momentum and is just about to emerge out of a consolidation pattern, such as a cup-with-handle or a flat base, which is a pattern we'll be looking at shortly. Firstly, though, take a look at two examples of buying a fund at the right time.

Buying at the right time

The first example is a fund called the Schroder UK Mid 250 A ACC.

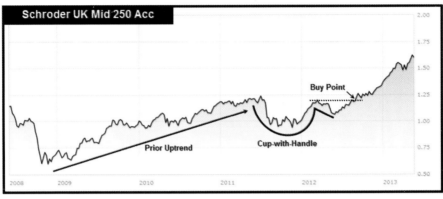

Chart courtesy of Morningstar.co.uk.

We purchased it on July 24th 2012 at a price of 1.31. Notice that we bought this after it had completed its cup-with-handle formation and just after buying, it took off like a rocket. In the first twelve months of owning it, this beauty surged 50.4%.

The Invesco Perpetual UK Growth ACC was purchased on the same day (July 24th 2012) as the Schroder fund, at a price of 3.41.

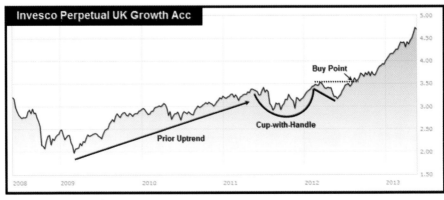

Chart courtesy of Morningstar.co.uk.

Notice once again that we bought it after it had completed its cup-with-handle formation. This darling also made a substantial move in the first twelve months that we owned it, vaulting 43.1%.

Flat base pattern

Though the cup-with-handle base is the most common pattern, there is another type of base to be on the lookout for, which is known as a flat base. Flat base patterns often form quietly, but the gains they launch can be explosive. These chart patterns frequently take shape when the broader market isn't making much upward progress.

Flat Base

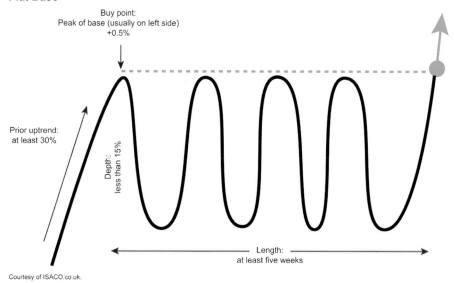

Courtesy of ISACO.co.uk.

Flat bases tend to be shallow – no deeper than 15% from top to bottom. And they can form in as little as five weeks, rather than the usual seven weeks required for cup-with-handle bases. Flat bases sometimes occur after a fund rushes up from a previous base, then stalls. As its price moves in a narrow sideways range, its base looks rather flat on a chart. In many cases, the fund is simply taking a break as it consolidates its gains and prepares to head higher.

Think of it as a time when the fund is building up steam to propel its future take-off. To calculate the buy point of a flat base, add 0.5% to the peak, which is usually on the base's left side. That 0.5% is just added assurance that the fund has enough emerging strength to get above its earlier price high.

Three flat base examples

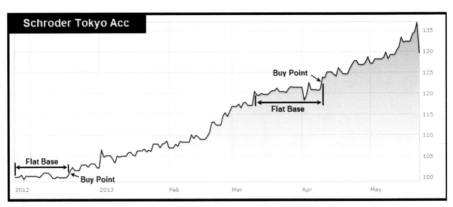

Chart courtesy of Morningstar.co.uk.

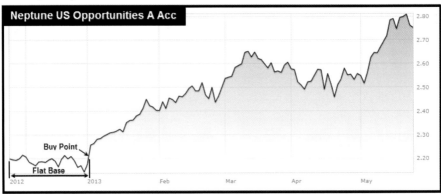

Chart courtesy of Morningstar.co.uk.

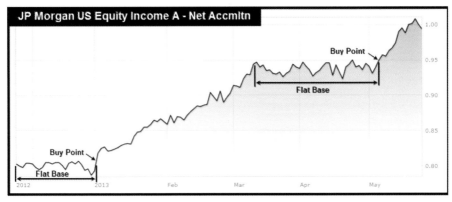

Chart courtesy of Morningstar.co.uk.

My take on stop losses

As you heard in **Chapter 1: My Story**, when I trade stocks I use stop losses. As a reminder, if a stock I own drops 7% below my buy price, I sell it. However, with funds I don't always use stop losses. One thing you have to be careful of when buying a fund is exit fees. Sometimes in a fund's Key Investor Information Document (KIID) you discover that it has an exit charge. If a fund does come with an exit charge, you sometimes see a clause in the KIID that states that any investor who decides to sell the fund within a 90-day period of buying it will be penalised.

Not all funds carry exit fees, however if the fund did come with an exit clause and you used a stop loss, you could get whacked with a hefty 5% fee. Trading on the Fidelity platform, we are fortunate enough to not suffer exit fees as they waive them on all the funds, however exit penalties are not the only reason I generally don't use stop losses when trading funds. Funds are a completely different animal to stocks and have to be treated differently.

They are not as risky as individual equities because a single stock could fall as much as 50% in one day and the most I've seen a fund drop in one day is about 8%. Stocks can tank and never come back because single businesses can go into liquidation overnight, however funds are different because they usually own anything from 30–100 stocks. This helps to provide the fund with diversification and it also helps to lower the risk.

If one of the stocks that the fund owns implodes, it's not likely to create a huge negative impact on the fund's value. Typically, funds only fall hard when all the stocks that the fund owns fall hard. And so for this reason, if the fund drops in price just after buying it, I usually hang on because the fall in price is typically due to the market experiencing a normal and natural correction.

When the market corrects, most funds correct and so, if I believe the retracement is normal and what I class as a healthy bull market correction, I'm prepared to give the fund room to breathe. My thinking is, I want to see how my new fund performs when the market eventually finds a floor and starts its next rally. If my fund was outperforming and therefore 'in' the money flow, I'd keep it but if it wasn't performing, I'd normally exit.

A stop loss would have cost me a gain of 64.9%

Here is an example of when I broke the rules and bought a fund when it was low in price.

After buying it on December 16th 2008 at a price of 2.14, it then proceeded to fall to a price of 1.78, which resulted in a 16.8% paper loss.

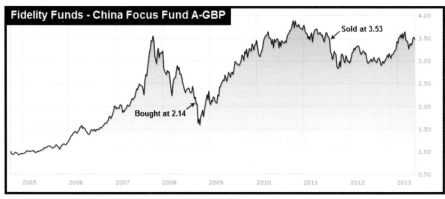

Chart courtesy of Morningstar.co.uk.

However, if I had adopted the 7% stop loss rule I use when buying stocks, I would have missed out on bagging a tidy gain of 64.9% over a 31 month period. For reference, I sold this fund at a price of 3.53 on July 27th 2011.

Now that we've covered all the key points associated with when to buy, we can now look at when to sell.

When to sell

What is the best way to determine whether you should keep hold of a fund? What signals or signs should you look out for, telling you that all is okay or whether something is wrong? The amateur way is to go by how you feel. I prefer to base my decision on three things: market direction, recent fund performance and the fund chart pattern.

1) Market direction

In the next chapter, you'll learn exactly how I read the health and direction of the market. This will prove to be a valuable skill to have in life, should you decide to acquire it. Knowing if the market is healthy is an extremely useful tool because if the market is in a bull phase, three out of four funds will move up, meaning it's a good time to be fully invested.

However, if the market is in a bear phase, three out of four funds are going to move down, which means it's not a good time to be invested in equity based funds. This tells you that when you have fully developed the skill of reading market direction, you'll be able to focus on investing in quality funds during bull markets and raising cash in bear markets.

2) Recent fund performance

I keep a close eye on how the funds I own are acting on a daily basis and I am constantly measuring to see how my fund is performing versus the market. Ideally, when the indexes rise, my fund will outperform the general market for the day and when the market falls, it will outperform on the downside too.

However, in reality this rarely happens so you have to look at the fund's weekly performance versus the market, its fortnightly performance and its monthly performance too. But don't stop there – also look at its 3 month, 6 month and 12 month performance. I always pay particular attention to how my funds behave when the indexes are rallying and ideally, they'll be making a greater return than the general market.

In a perfect world, the fund should be beating the market and if it isn't, a red flag should be raised. If it is doing better than the market, it tells you that it's probably best to hold onto it but if it isn't, and its underperformance is over a significant period of time such as 3–12 months, it usually means that it's time to sell.

Another thing that I do which is worth sharing is watch how the stocks the fund owns are performing on a daily basis. I do this by setting up watchlists on MarketSmith (more about MarketSmith in **Chapter 10: How to Manage Your Portfolio**), which is a paid for subscription and Yahoo! Finance, which is free.

Each day I look at how the stocks the fund owns are behaving and if they are beating the market, it tells me all is well, which gives me the green light to stay invested. However, if I see the stocks constantly underperforming, it tells me that it might be time to ditch the fund.

3) Chart pattern

Periodically, I like to check the fund's chart pattern. Why? I want to make sure it's acting right and ideally beating the market. For example, if the market is correcting, the fund might instead be moving sideways rather than carving out a big bowl shape – that's a sign of strength. On the flip side, if the market is advancing and I see that the chart of my fund shows it's been shuffling sideways, that's a sign that it might be time to exit.

It's also good to be aware of certain bearish chart patterns that funds carve out prior to them breaking down, such as climax tops and head and shoulder patterns. A climax top occurs when a fund rises very quickly and gets overextended. During a climax top, funds can make enormous gains in a very short period of time (usually less than two weeks). As an investor you certainly don't want to be one of the last passengers on the train and get quickly thrown off.

In the next chapter, you'll see a fund called the Legg Mason Japan Equity A Acc – a fund that we owned which experienced a climax top. The head and shoulders pattern is generally regarded as a reversal pattern and it is most often seen in uptrends. I recommend you Google the term 'climax top' and 'head and shoulder pattern' to discover lots of examples of what these two bearish chart patterns look like.

Selling signals

Always know what stocks your fund owns and monitor those stocks closely. Are the stocks the fund owns breaking down? Is the fund as a whole underperforming the market? Ask yourself the question, would I buy this fund right now? If you wouldn't, get rid of it. Never fall in love with a fund and if it's been underperforming for some time, exit it and don't look back.

Selling an underperforming weak fund you own can be tough. You start to play mind games with yourself and worry that after you sell it, it's going to make a huge move to the upside. This by the way, rarely happens. Weak funds tend to get weaker and strong funds tend to get stronger. The psychological trick I use to get around this is to remind myself that I can always get back into a fund at a later date, should it come back to life in the future. This gives me the reassurance that I'm not going to miss out if it makes a major move to the upside.

More tips on buying and selling funds

To achieve success, it's important to have clear objectives. For example, one of my goals is to buy a fund that will outperform the market and sell it when it's been underperforming over a significant amount of time. I always like to be aware what market cycle we are in and whether it's a bull or a bear cycle. If we are in a bull market I remain fully invested but in bear markets I raise cash.

As I mentioned before, you'll learn exactly how to analyse the market and determine what cycle we are in when you read the next chapter. Try to adopt an attitude of constant learning and if you really want to get good at knowing when to buy and when to exit funds, read as many books as you can on technical analysis and investment psychology. I also suggest that you make a habit of analysing each and every trade you make and trying to learn from your mistakes.

The easy route

However, if you don't have the time or intention to learn how to improve the buying and selling of your funds, you could take the easy route and get some expert guidance from people who know what they are doing. Subscribe to services that will help you become a better trader and never delegate the investment process to a person or company – ever. Instead, I recommend you always keep full control of your investment decisions but seek out experts who can provide guidance rather than specific and personalised advice.

Aim to find a person or company that you can invest with side by side. I suggest you attend as many reputable investment seminars as you can and subscribe to the best investment blogs you can find. The key is to continue to keep upgrading your skills and knowledge throughout your life and always learn from investors with proven track records.

My friend, it's now time to learn the secrets of how the pros gauge stock market direction. As you've heard on numerous occasions, most stocks and funds move in the same direction as the general market and that means from this point onwards you need to trade with the trend and not against it. If you trade with it, you won't go far wrong but if you try to fight the trend, you are going to get hurt.

By the time you've finished the next chapter you'll understand how to analyse the market's health and direction, why you need to keep a close eye on the behaviour of leading stocks and how to protect yourself from market downturns. But we're not going to stop there – I'm also going to show you how to identify market tops, how to spot market bottoms and additional ways to pick up on key market turning points. Sound good? I hope so, because it's time to discover everything you need to know about…

8: Gauging Stock Market Direction

'One useful fact to remember is that the most important indications are made in the early stages of a broad market move. Nine times out of ten the leaders of an advance are the stocks that make new highs ahead of the averages.'
– Gerald M. Loeb

Even if you have a real knack for picking the best fund, if you are wrong about the trend of the market, your portfolio is going to suffer. This happened to thousands of uninformed investors in the great bear markets of 2000–2002 and 2007–2009. Many investors mistakenly think that it is all about choosing the best investments to park their money in.

While finding quality investments is important, it's not as crucial as getting in sync with the market's trend and direction. This means it's essential that you have a reliable method of determining which way the market is heading. And, if your desire is to become really good at this, it is going to take time and plenty of hard work. Throughout your investment journey, you will ideally need to know if we are in a bull (up) or a bear (down) market.

Is the market healthy or unhealthy?

If we are in a bull market, are we are in the early or later stages? I've found that to win with investing, you have to watch what the market is doing and interpret what it means. For example, is the market behaving well? Or is it weak and acting out of character? To achieve investment success, it helps if you have a good handle on the market's current health and likely future direction.

The best way I've found of achieving this is to watch what the general market averages are doing on a daily basis. In his bestselling book, *How to Make Money in Stocks*, William O'Neil said: 'Don't let anyone tell you that you can't time the market'. According to O'Neil, the mistaken belief that no one can time the market evolved more than 30 years ago when most funds that tried it were unsuccessful.

This is because they had to buy and sell at exactly the right time but due to their asset size problems, it took weeks to raise cash and weeks to re-enter the market. Therefore, the top management at these funds imposed rules on their fund managers that required them to remain fully invested (95–100% of assets)[34].

Can the market be timed?

Even though a stock market legend like William O'Neil says that it is possible to time the market, opinions are divided on this highly debatable topic. My belief is that the market can be timed – although it is extremely difficult and to always get it right is impossible. In the 2003–2007 bull market, we used a tactical timing approach.

This approach involved attempting to exit the market every time it experienced a correction. Our aim was to spot intermediate market tops and move into cash. We made many mistakes and it really was a costly lesson, which resulted in underperformance. We like to learn from our mistakes however, and when something is not working, we change it.

Strategic timing is more effective

Since 2008, we've used a strategic timing approach and it's proved to have been far more effective. Strategic timing is less frequent than tactical timing and involves staying fully invested during bull market phases. The goal is to get out of the market into cash once the bull market has finished its run. This is when we believe a major downtrend has been triggered and a new bear market has begun.

During the bull phase, we normally make no more than four switches to our portfolio each year. During bull markets, our goal is to identify which areas, sectors and countries the big money is flowing into and invest in them. This means that during a bull phase we make switches out of any funds that show underperformance into ones that we believe offer greater growth potential. This change has resulted in outperformance during this latest bull market.

Sometimes you just have to be honest with yourself when something isn't working, admit to yourself that you've made a mistake and then make a change. Hopefully, by sharing this with you, you won't make the same mistake we made and try to time the market too frequently. Now it's time to look at how to read and analyse the market. If you buy into our thinking, each and every day, your job will be to try to determine the stock market's health. To do this, you simply observe and study the major indexes carefully.

We do this by tracking and analysing the following US indexes:

- The NASDAQ Composite
- The S&P 600
- The S&P 500
- The Dow Jones Industrial Average

Even though we like to keep an eye on all the world exchanges, our main focus has always been on the US markets and, as a reminder, there are four reasons why we do this:

1) The US is the world's largest economy
2) The US is the leading market to watch for clues of future direction
3) The US stock market indexes long-term growth exceeds other world exchanges
4) My philosophy involves watching the behaviour of US institutional investors

The other indexes around the world that we watch are the FTSE 100, the Nikkei 225, the SSE Composite, the BSE SENSEX and the Russian Trading System (RTS). As well as watching the four main US indexes, we believe it's crucial to watch the behaviour of the US's leading stocks and leading sectors. By studying these four indexes, plus the action of leading stocks and sectors, each and every day, you can keep a close eye on the market's *character* and quickly notice any significant changes in the market's 'personality', which can help you to spot market tops and bottoms.

Is buy and hold broken?

Buy and hold is an investment strategy that only tends to work in long-term upward trending markets, such as the super bull market that occurred between 1980 and the year 2000. Unfortunately, the market does not always go up, as many investors have experienced over the last twelve years.

And if you did decide to take a buy and hold approach, you still have the difficult task of correctly timing your initial buy. A buy and hold strategy may work, but only if you buy when the market is low and just before a bull market begins. But what about during bear markets? Adhering to a buy and hold program during significant correction periods can be very painful, particularly if retirement is approaching.

Why we prefer strategic timing

Another reason why we prefer strategic timing is because every buy and hold program has to start with an initial buy. You have to decide when to get in and if your decision is based on emotions, which it usually is, you may encounter problems. For example, if you had used a buy and hold strategy and bought at the peak of 2000, just before the 2000–2002 savage bear market, or at the 2007 top, just before the 2007–2009 financial crisis, you may have experienced losses of 50–90%.

Dropping 50% requires a 100% gain to get you back to even. In the 2000–2002 bear market, my ISA account dropped 27.3%, which was pretty good when you consider that the FTSE 100 over the same period made a loss of 43.2%. The NASDAQ Composite did even worse, imploding by 67.2%.

However, in the most recent bear market of 2007 to 2009, I wasn't so lucky. In 2008, the FTSE 100 fell 31.3%, the NASDAQ tumbled 40.5% and my account sunk by 42.3%. Fortunately, my portfolio rebounded strongly – I made a 56.4% gain in 2009 and 27.2% in 2010, which helped to make the loss back quickly.

But others who experienced significant losses during 2008 won't have been as lucky. Some investors who took heavy falls will be sitting in those losses for up to a decade. Imagine what it must be like for those investors who took a loss of 90% in either of those two bear markets. For them it would mean their portfolio having to rise 900% to get back to where they started. That could take some time! The table explains how this works.

Size of loss (%)	Gain (%) needed to get back to even
33	50
50	100
90	900

Courtesy of ISACO.co.uk.

This is why it is so important for you to try to preserve your capital and get out of the market and into the safety of cash when you see the first signs that the market has changed from healthy to unhealthy.

Most investors buy at the wrong time

You might be thinking that you'd have to be extremely unlucky to buy right at the top of the market, however, as you will soon see, unfortunately most investors do buy at the wrong time. The perfect point to start a buy and hold program is right at the bottom of the market and the point to exit would be right at the top.

The challenge we all face is that when the market is at its bottom, not many people feel like starting their buy and hold program. Most investors want to start their buy and hold strategy when the market is at its top – again because of how they feel. Unfortunately, all too often investors are influenced by short-term market movements rather than focusing on the longer term trend.

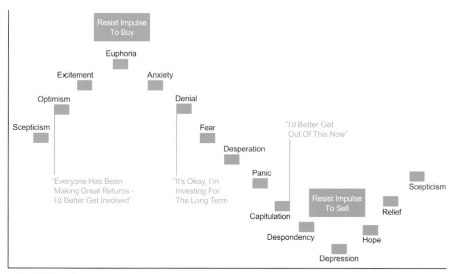

Courtesy of ISACO.co.uk.

As the chart illustrates, many investors go through a range of emotions at different points in a market cycle. All too often this can result in them entering or exiting the market at precisely the wrong time.

As markets peak, investors experience emotions of excitement, thrill and euphoria. This tempts unsuspecting buy and hold investors to start their programs when the market is highly priced. But, as markets dip, negative emotions of panic, despondency and depression lead buy and hold investors to give up on their plan, exit the market and realise a loss.

Buying high and selling low

To support this theory, the next chart shows historic net investment flows (investment purchases minus investment sales by retail clients) into equity funds by UK investors, alongside movements of the FTSE 100 Index, between 1992 and 2009.

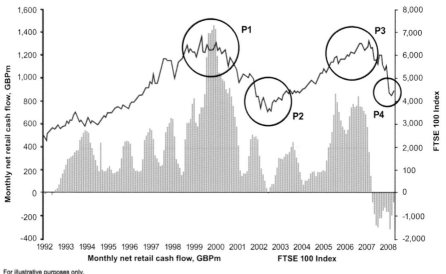

For illustrative purposes only.
Source: IMA, MSCI. Monthly cash flow data shown reflects 6 month moving average.

As can be seen, investment flows increase significantly as markets peak, especially during P1 in 2000 and P3 in 2006/2007, and conversely decrease during market dips, especially during P2 in 2002 and P4 in 2008, when we see net outflows (i.e. more sales than purchases by investors) from funds.

Successful fund selection is all in the timing

Let's now look at the dangers associated with buy and hold, using a real life example of a fund we bought back in 2005 and what would have happened to our clients' accounts if we hadn't taken a more active role. The fund we bought was called the *Legg Mason Japan Equity A*.

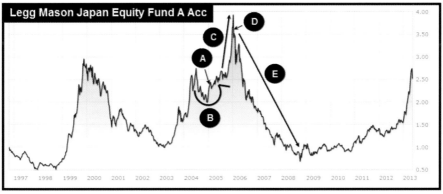

Chart courtesy of Morningstar.co.uk.

We bought this fund at a price of 2.32 on January 11th 2005 (Point A), just before it broke out of a bullish cup-with-handle formation (Point B). Soon after purchase, this fund really took off, eventually hitting a peak at 3.93. We recognised this behaviour as climax topping (Point C) and, soon after it hit this high, we decided to exit at a price of 3.32 (Point D) on January 5th 2006. This helped us net a 43.1% gain in twelve months. As you can see from the chart, just after getting out, the fund fell like a stone, dropping 71.4% (Point E) over the next three years.

Aim to stay fully invested during bull markets

Buy and hold could work if you started your program at the right time but as you've seen, unfortunately most investors don't buy at the optimum point. You could of course decide to adopt a pound cost averaging strategy, a strategy we use for investing capital outside an ISA and SIPP, and we'll be exploring how that method works in **Chapter 11: Creating an Income for Life**.

I'm sure you already know this but just in case, pound cost averaging is the practice of investing a predetermined amount of money at regular intervals, regardless of market conditions. The amount you invest is constant, so you buy more shares when the price is low and fewer when the price is high. Adopting such an approach could help you avoid the risk of mistiming your initial buy. Even though this is a better approach, it makes more sense when investing using ISAs and SIPPs to consider becoming more active and aiming to strategically time the market.

We've found that overtrading cuts into your returns, just as trying to time the market too frequently is extremely difficult to execute on a consistent basis. During a bull market we'll normally make no more than four trades each year and our changes are triggered when we see underperformance from a fund we own. This happens due to sector rotation, which is when money moves from one sector into another.

Watching where the big money is flowing

For example, technology may be the hot sector for a while but eventually it has to cool off. As it cools, the big money flows into the next hot sector, for example, financials. These hot sectors are known as leading sectors and all leading sectors eventually become laggards. This is why it's important to keep a close eye on which sectors are leading and which ones are lagging and as I mentioned in the last chapter, never fall in love with an investment you own.

The aim is to keep track of the money flow and to try and always be positioned right in the middle of the money flow during a bull phase. This is easier said than done of course, but it still should be your aim. When a bull market is over, and you believe a downtrend has been triggered, you could move into cash and stay in cash during the full length of the bear market.

Making better and more accurate timing decisions starts with understanding how the stock markets operate in cycles and how the majority of the daily trading volume is created by institutional involvement – large investors who have a significant influence on the market's trend and direction.

Do fundamentals still matter?

In 2003, the FTSE 100 bottomed at 3392 and in 2009, it hit a low of 3461. Who would have thought that the FTSE 100 would revisit a similar price point again? Between 2008 and 2009, some of world's most respected companies lost as much as 90% of their share value and that's the reason why we all may need to look beyond fundamentals. Technical analysis is different to looking at fundamentals. It looks at chart trends and asks the question, is the market in an uptrend or a downtrend?

Is technical analysis the solution?

While technical analysis is not a perfect solution, it can often provide an effective way to help you gauge market direction. It can also remove the emotional element of stock market investing. Fundamentally, you can look at corporate profits, GDP growth, unemployment, inflation and price/earnings ratios to try to determine if the general market is under or overvalued.

Adding technical analysis to your tool box aims to keep you invested when trends are up. On the other hand, it also aims to get you out of the market when major downtrends have been triggered. Before you decide to invest, you could ask – is the market and the fund I'm thinking of buying in an uptrend? If the trend is up, you would have more confidence issuing a buy order.

If the trend is down, you may decide to remain in cash until an uptrend has been established. In a down market, even funds run by star-performing fund managers follow the same direction as the market – just one of the reasons why we aim to park in cash during bear markets.

Why it pays to watch indexes more than economic data

Did you know that the market is six month forward-looking? This means that you are going to struggle gauging future market direction if you use the news headlines and economic indicators to guide you. Using the news headlines and economic data to guide your investment decisions doesn't work because the market will have already factored all the news and data into its current price.

If you find the countless economic indicators confusing, join the club! How are you supposed to know if an industrial production figure is good or bad? How should you interpret the jobs report? I've found that economic gauges reflect the past or, at their best, the present. They won't really tell you the future. Often, by the time the economy starts cooling, stocks and investment funds will have already suffered a downturn.

Likewise, a new uptrend can emerge while economic activity is slumping, or even as the economic cycle is at its worst point. There are two headlines that we pay attention to. The first is 'Federal Reserve Raises Rates' and the second is, 'Federal Reserve Lowers Rates'. The Federal Reserve is the US's equivalent of the Bank of England and one of the Fed's jobs is to decide if interest rates need to be changed. Interest rates are crucial to economic activity, and to the stock market. The stock market loves rate cuts and hates rate increases.

Did you know that the stock market has a personality?

The stock market can behave in different ways. Sometimes its personality is friendly and the market's the best friend you could ever ask for. Other times however, the market's like the bully from hell who beats you up and steals your lunch. Funds have a personality and so do stocks. In bull markets, they tend to act well. In bear markets, they turn tail and drop like stones from the sky.

The only way to know if the behaviour of the market, stocks or your fund is normal is by watching their activity extremely closely. For indexes and stocks, this means watching the action whilst the market is open and analysing the market once it's closed. Funds don't trade in real time and so their behaviour needs to be analysed after the market is closed. You have to put in the time to really get to know the personality and character of the market so that when something changes you'll know and you'll be able to react quickly.

Market indexes always eventually move into higher ground

Did you know that the market indexes always eventually move into higher ground? Sometimes they do move sideways for very long periods (a decade or more) but eventually they always break into new high ground. The most popular market index in the UK is the FTSE 100, which you are probably familiar with but have you heard of the S&P 500? The FTSE 100 is an index that contains the hundred largest publicly traded companies in the UK and the S&P 500 is the United States equivalent, and contains five hundred of the largest US businesses.

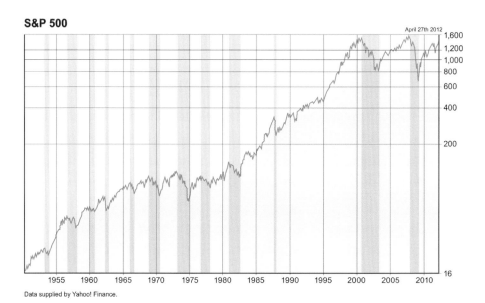

S&P 500

April 27th 2012

Data supplied by Yahoo! Finance.

As you can see from the illustration, the long-term trend that the S&P 500 has formed is up. Look closely and you'll notice that the chart features grey vertical shaded areas and these represent the bear markets. The white areas on this chart are the bull markets.

If you take another look, you'll also notice that apart from the two most recent bear markets, the market has always recovered after significant correction periods and proceeded to move into new higher ground. This means that, at some point in the future, indexes such as the S&P 500 will eventually make new highs, far and above the highs made on October 11th 2007, when it topped out at 1,576.09. In fact, as I write this, it's currently trading at 1472^{35}, just 7% below its October 2007 high.

The market works in cycles

Bull markets last between two and four years. Bear markets last approximately nine to eighteen months. Because bull markets last longer, the stock market over the long term forms an uptrend. In a typical cycle, you'd normally have three years up and then one year down. The bull/bear cycle then starts again and keeps repeating.

Bear markets tend to end when businesses and the economy are still in a downturn and bull markets often end way before a recession sets in and usually when all the business and economic data looks positive. The market's action is determined by millions of investors and its daily activity is a result of the investors' general consensus about what they like or don't like and what they foresee happening in the world. For example, what governments are doing or about to do and what the consequences of those actions could be.

Make money by asking the audience

Rather than trying to work out where the market is likely to head by reading reams of economic data, reading the newspaper or listening to the latest financial news, we would rather see what institutional investors think and more importantly, closely watch what they are doing. We can very easily see what they are thinking by looking at charts. We can tell if they are bullish and aggressively buying stock or if they are bearish and aggressively selling.

Each and every day we simply analyse what has happened and what it means. We look to see if it is positive, neutral or negative. If, over several weeks, the activity is positive, it would tell you that the market is behaving well and therefore more likely to head north than south. If, however, the behaviour is negative, it would suggest that the market is more likely to head south.

How to analyse the market's health

Institutions, not individuals, account for nearly 75% of the daily trading activity on the exchanges[36]. That's why it's important to watch their activity carefully. The large institutional investors have the greatest influence on the stock market and consist of investment funds, banks, pension funds and insurance companies.

If these 800lb gorilla investors are buying, smaller, more nimble investors like you and me can jump onto their coat-tails. And if these institutional investors are selling, you could quickly switch out on to the sidelines. Here is how it works. Picture the market as a large tree and try to imagine institutional investors being woodcutters. If institutional investors are selling heavily it is as if they are taking a cut out of the tree and this of course, makes the tree weaker.

If they take too many swipes at the tree in a short space of time, what is going to happen? That's right, the tree will fall over. This means that the market gets weak when it succumbs to excessive selling, which results in a red flag being raised. When heavy selling occurs, especially over a short period of time, it's often a sign to say that it's probably the time to get out of the market. On the other hand, when institutional investors are buying heavily over a short period of time, it makes the market healthy and extremely strong, and this is the time we like to be invested.

Why it pays to watch the price and volume action

One of the best ways of reading the market's health and gauging its likely future direction is to look at charts. A stock chart is a graph that displays the price and volume history of a given security or index over a period of days, months or years. Price and volume charts help you to see what the professional investors are doing; allowing you the opportunity to follow in the large investors' footsteps.

Institutional investors cannot hide their tracks. Think of an elephant getting into a bathtub. Whether they are buying or selling, through a chart you can clearly see what the big players are doing. Price action is how a stock or index changes in price. Volume action is the number of shares traded.

In the volume part of the chart, notice the red horizontal moving line.

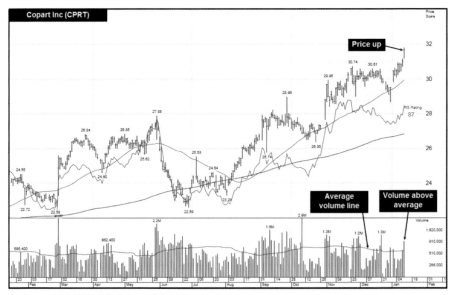

This represents the average volume levels over the previous 50 days. If trading volume is above average and price action is up, institutional investors are buying. That's good. This is classed as healthy behaviour.

On the other hand, if volume is above average and price action is down, it means institutional investors are selling. That's not good. This is classed as unhealthy behaviour.

If volume is below average and the price action is up, it indicates little demand from institutional investors. That's also not good. This is seen as unhealthy behaviour.

And finally, if volume is below average and the price action is down, it indicates that institutional investors are reluctant to sell. This type of action is good. This is seen as healthy behaviour.

It does take a lot of buying or selling to change an established trend. By carefully analysing the market's behaviour on a daily basis, it can assist you in trying to determine whether the trend has changed. If you believe it has, you can act accordingly. If, after analysis, you thought the trend was up, you would invest.

However, if you believed the market's trend was down, you could park in cash. By watching the trading activity closely, you can see exactly what institutional investors are doing with their money – effectively allowing you to get in sync, and trade with the trend, instead of against it.

Reading the market every day could reap you a fortune

I suggest you aim to make it a habit of reading the market day in, day out. It's important to read and analyse the market this regularly because a piece of positive or negative news could change the whole market dynamic in just a single day. How the market responds to the news will ultimately govern how you react. The market's health and direction could alter in the space of 24 hours, which is why you should remain vigilant at all times. If you take your eye off the market, you may miss out on the opportunity of getting in when a new uptrend has been established.

When you get in early, you have the potential to profit from exciting investment opportunities but when you fail to get in early you could miss out on strong investment returns over relatively short time frames. Another reason to read the market every day is to avoid getting locked into a falling market when a downtrend has been triggered. This could result in unnecessary loss – that could have been avoided by being a more diligent follower of index, stock and sector activity.

Why it pays to watch what the big players are doing

By making it a habit to read the market every day, five days a week, you'll be able to make a good call on its health. By reviewing the behaviour of the market over the previous several weeks, and the activity that day, you'll be able to decide if it is in an uptrend and healthy, or in a downtrend and unhealthy. If you class the market as being healthy, it means you'll probably be invested.

On the other hand, if you believe the market to be unhealthy, you will be able to temporarily park in cash. The stance you take on the market can be created by daily analysis of the market indexes and leading stocks. Your in-depth intraday look at the market could be followed by a thorough after-market check up. The concluding results could then be reported in your own personal trading diary.

How to spot stock market tops

Historically, market tops occur after the averages move into new high ground and show several days of large and increased volume, with either very poor price progress or actual declines in the averages. A series of distribution days (institutional selling) mark the end of a bull market.

A distribution day occurs when one of the major stock indexes falls on above average volume. When the market piles up four or five distribution days in just a few weeks, and the uptrend seems to have stalled, chances are it's heading into a correction, especially when you notice many top stocks falling heavily in great volume.

The best time to bank a profit

If you believe that the market's major trend has changed from up to down, you can bank some or all of your profits by switching out of your equity based fund investments and moving into cash. When investing in stocks and shares ISAs, be aware that it's not about selling (withdrawing money from your ISA) – it's about switching (keeping the money invested in the ISA wrapper). By parking your money in cash on a temporary basis, it means that even if the market crashes, your money will be safe.

In fact, although equity ISAs could be dropping like stones, a Cash Park will actually be rising in value. After moving into cash, you simply sit, wait and remain patient. Many investors don't realise that it is possible to park in cash. Some mistakenly think that once you are invested in a fund, you have to stay in that fund. Some wrongly think that to switch into a Cash Park would adversely affect their annual allowance – it doesn't.

Why it's smart to keep a close eye on leading stocks

Throughout the year, come rain or shine, I love to watch the daily activity of the market's best stocks. The reason I watch them like a hawk is because they tend to lead the market higher or lower – before the general market catches on.

This means that they are a very good indicator of which direction the market is likely to head next. For example, back in 1999 during the technology bubble, leading stocks at the time were equities such as Yahoo! and Microsoft. As you can see on this 20 year chart of the NASDAQ Composite, the general market topped in March 2000.

The market may have topped in March 2000, however Microsoft (ticker symbol: MSFT), a leading stock at the time, topped in December 1999, giving investors a signal that the bull market might be close to a top.

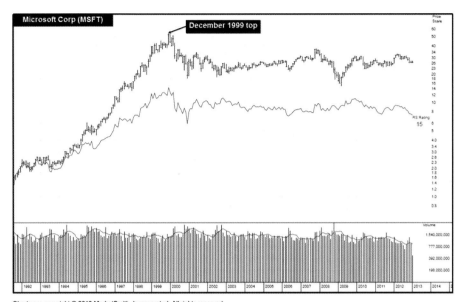

Yahoo! (ticker symbol: YHOO), another leader at the time, topped in January 2000, which was another clue that a top was coming.

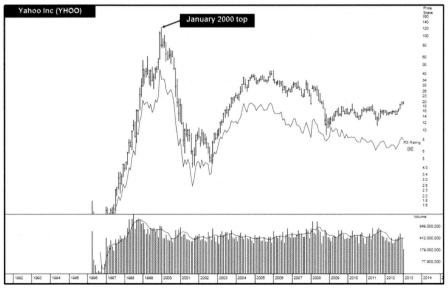

As I mentioned, it also happens on the flip side too. Stocks such as Rio Tinto (ticker symbol: RIO) and BHP Billiton (ticker symbol: BHP) were two of the leading stocks at the start of the bull market that began in 2009.

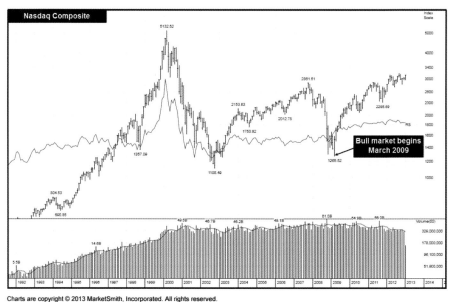

It's interesting to note therefore, that BHP Billiton (see chart on page 159) bottomed in November 2008, four months before the market turned around.

It's also interesting to see Rio Tinto (see chart on page 159) another leader in 2009 and 2010, bottoming out in December 2008, which was three months before the 2009 bull market began.

It's also good to know that a leading stock can become a laggard stock. Personally, I class a leading stock as one that has an RS (relative strength) rating on MarketSmith of 80 or above and an EPS (earnings per share) rating of 80 or above.

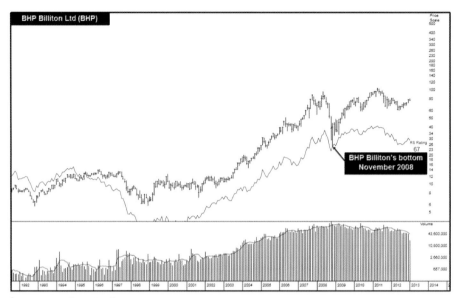

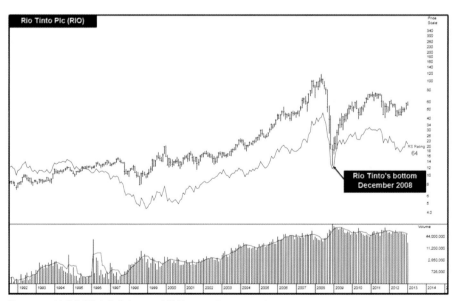

You'll discover more about MarketSmith in **Chapter 10: How to Manage Your Portfolio**. Stocks' ratings change on a daily basis, which means it's probably a good idea to always have a list of stocks that you class as leaders and continually work on adding new members to the list and removing stocks that no longer match your leading stock criteria.

How to spot a stock market bottom

So, how do you know when a market correction has hit bottom? We keep our eye on a number of things, such as the behaviour of the US indexes, the activity and personality of leading stocks and we also look for a follow-through day. This is a day that helps to confirm that institutional investors are going all in. The follow-through is a concept coined by William O'Neil and can be summarised as follows: you look for an increase in total market volume from the day before and substantial price progress for the day, up at least 1.7% or more in any index.

We like to see a follow-through occur on either the NASDAQ Composite or S&P 600. The phenomenon of a follow-through day has occurred in every new bull market throughout history, though not all follow-through days result in a new bull market. A follow-through on the fourth day or later of an attempted rally is likely to be an indicator of follow-through buying from institutions with conviction. A first, second, or third-day rally attempt off a market bottom can often be little more than short-covering.

Gold nuggets

As you've discovered, observing how the general averages are acting is essential in helping you gauge the market's future trend or direction. However, there are some key indicators that can give you a head start when spotting market turning points. One of the things that we like to see happening to confirm that the market is strong and vibrant, is the way that the NASDAQ Composite, the NASDAQ 100 and the chip sector are acting.

We refer to the NASDAQ 100 as the NASDAQ Composite's big brother. The NASDAQ 100 is formed of the 100 largest stocks listed on the NASDAQ Composite and includes giants such as Microsoft, Google and Cisco Systems. Chips are a common term for semiconductors. The main index for chips is the PHLX Semiconductor and is commonly known as the SOX.

A giant magnet

If the market is rising but being led by the Dow or the S&P 500, meaning that the NASDAQ Composite, the NASDAQ 100 and the chip sector are lagging, it means that the rally (uptrend) is more prone to fail. But if the NASDAQ Composite, the NASDAQ 100 and the chip sector are leading the market higher, it tells you that the rally is more likely to succeed. By watching the market every single day, we've noticed that these three key indicators act like a kind of giant magnet.

In other words, when they are weak, they tend to pull and lead the market down, but when they are strong they tend to pull and lead the market up. We like to watch the NASDAQ 100's action in two ways. We look at the chart of the NASDAQ 100 and we look at the chart of the QQQs, which is the exchange traded fund (ETF) that tracks the movement of the 100. By watching the QQQs, we can carefully study the behaviour of the NASDAQ 100.

With chips, we like to watch the SOX and the SMH, which is the exchange traded fund that tracks the performance of a number of major semiconductor companies. Included in the SMH are Intel, Texas Instruments and Applied Materials. The NASDAQ Composite, the NASDAQ 100 and the chip sector are three key indicators that can give you early signals to act. We watch them very closely and I suggest you do too.

How to read the market like a professional

The market has worked in exactly the same way since it began in the late 1800s. It is always about supply and demand, and the way to analyse supply and demand is through looking at price and volume behaviour on charts. Institutional investors can be bullish one minute but then discover some new information that overrides their optimistic outlook. At the end of the day, to read the market effectively, you have to remember that it really does not matter what is happening news wise. Regardless of what the news or any market commentator is saying, if the price and volume action is positive, then that's good, period. And that goes for the downside too.

If all the news headlines are positive but the market's behaviour is saying the opposite, then you had better be thinking about switching into the safety of cash. The lesson here is simple. Do not look to the news or economic data to tell you what is going on or going to happen. Instead, find out what is really going on by studying the daily market activity using stock charts.

Phew, that was a lot of information to take on board, but I'm sure you found it to be extremely helpful. I'm also thinking that everything is probably starting to make more sense and click into place. If it is, great! Okay, now that you've learned the valuable skill of how to gauge stock market direction, we can now delve into the fascinating subject of behavioural finance. Don't let the stuffy term 'behavioural finance' put you off.

Basically it's a fancy way of saying 'investment psychology'. If like me, you are fascinated by human behaviour and how most of us can sometimes behave in odd and irrational ways, you are going to love this next chapter. I'm certain that when reading it, you will be able to relate many of the things I'm talking about to either yourself or another investor you know. It's time to go…

9: Beyond Greed and Fear

'The time of maximum pessimism is the best time to buy and the time of maximum optimism is the best time to sell.'
– Sir John Templeton

In this chapter we are going to look at how understanding behavioural finance can help you make better investment decisions and the process starts with getting a good grip on your financial personality. The key is to try becoming aware of the decisions you make and how you are likely to react to the uncertainty that comes with investing in the stock market. Understanding your financial personality can also help to control the irrational and illogical elements of your investment decisions.

Human nature usually serves us well in coping with day-to-day life. But it can also get in the way of achieving success in long-term activities, such as saving and investing. There is no cure for human nature, but a greater awareness of investment psychology can help you avoid major pitfalls.

According to accepted financial theory, human beings are rational (of sound mind). However, researchers have uncovered a surprisingly large amount of evidence that this is frequently not the case. Dozens of examples of irrational behaviour and repeated errors of judgment have been documented. The late Peter L. Bernstein wrote in *'Against The Gods'* that the evidence 'reveals repeated patterns of irrationality, inconsistency, and incompetence in the ways human beings arrive at decisions and choices when faced with uncertainty'.

Behavioural finance = investment psychology

The academic field of finance has long had a behavioural side. One of the classic examinations of irrational investor behaviour, '*Extraordinary Popular Delusions and the Madness of Crowds*', dates back to the 19th century. In the 1930s, legendary economist John Maynard Keynes and value-investing guru Benjamin Graham spoke of the effect of investors' emotions on stock prices. More recently, in 1982, money manager David Dreman published '*The New Contrarian Investment Strategy*', which argued that investors could outperform by not following market fads.

Modern portfolio theory is nonsense

The financial principles based on Modern Portfolio Theory (MPT)[37] and the Capital Asset Pricing Model (CAPM)[38] have long shaped the way in which many investors judge investment performance.

The theory is based on the belief that investors act rationally and consider all available information in the decision-making process and as a result, investment markets are efficient and have factored all available information into the prices of investments. However, researchers have uncovered a surprisingly large amount of evidence of irrationality and repeated errors of judgement.

A field of behavioural finance has evolved that attempts to better understand and explain how emotions influence investors and their decision-making process. Daniel Kahneman, Amos Tversky, Hersh Shefrin, Meir Statman, Robert Shiller and Andrei Shleifer are among the leading researchers who have used theories of psychology to shine some light on the accuracy of financial markets, and explain stock market bubbles and crashes.

People frequently behave irrationally

One of the most basic assumptions that accepted finance makes is that people are rational. According to conventional finance, emotions and other factors do not influence people when it comes to making financial choices.

But the fact is, people frequently behave irrationally. For example, consider how many people purchase lottery tickets in the hope of hitting the jackpot. From a purely logical standpoint, it does not make sense to buy a lottery ticket when the odds of winning are overwhelming against the ticket holder (roughly 1 in 14 million for the National Lottery jackpot). Despite this, millions of people in the UK buy tickets week in, week out.

Anomalies

Despite strong evidence that the stock market is highly efficient, there have been scores of studies that have documented long-term historical anomalies (irregularities) in the stock market that seem to go against the efficient market hypothesis. While the existence of irregularities is generally well accepted, the question of whether you can use them to earn impressive returns in the future is subject to debate. Let's now look at an example of one such anomaly; the winners curse.

The winner's curse

One assumption found in finance and economics is that investors and traders are rational enough to be aware of the true value of an asset and will bid or pay accordingly. However, anomalies such as the winner's curse – a tendency for the winning bid in an auction to be higher than the true value of the item purchased – suggest that this is not the case. Rational-based theories assume that all people involved in the bidding process at an auction will have access to all of the relevant information and will all come to the same valuation.

Any differences in the pricing would suggest that some other factor, not directly tied to the asset, is affecting the bidding. According to Robert Thaler's 1988 article on the winner's curse, there are two primary factors that weaken the rational bidding process: the number of bidders and the aggressiveness of the bidding.

For example, the more bidders involved in the process means that you have to bid more aggressively in order to put others off from bidding. Unfortunately, increasing your aggressiveness will also increase the likelihood that your winning bid will exceed the value of the asset.

Anchoring

Just as a house should be built upon a good, solid foundation, our ideas and opinions should also be based on correct facts in order to be considered valid. However, this is not always so. Anchoring is one of the root psychological flaws that pushes otherwise brilliant people to make financial mistakes and causes individuals to cling to a belief that may or may not be true, and to base their decisions for the future on that belief.

The inactivity that this leads to can have negative effects on their retirement accounts. For instance, if people anchor themselves to the belief that the stock market will keep going up, they will not only suffer from inactivity, they'll be putting themselves at risk when the market eventually turns.

A diamond anchor

Consider this classic example taken from Investopedia.com: Conventional wisdom states that a diamond engagement ring should cost around two months worth of salary. This standard is a wonderful example of anchoring and illustrates why most of us make illogical and irrational financial decisions. While spending two months worth of salary can serve as a benchmark, it is a completely irrelevant reference point created by the jewellery industry to maximize profits, and not a valuation of love.

Many men can't afford to set aside two months' salary towards an engagement ring while paying for living expenses. Consequently, a large number go into debt in order to meet the standard. In many cases, the diamond anchor will live up to its name, as the prospective groom struggles to keep his head above water in a sea of mounting debt.

Although the amount spent on an engagement ring should be dictated by what a person can afford, many men illogically anchor their decision to the two-month standard. Because buying jewellery is an unusual experience for many men, they are more likely to purchase something that is around the standard, despite the expense. This is the power of anchoring.

Common mistakes investors make

One anchoring behaviour that presents itself amongst investors is a reluctance to part with poorly performing investments. Often investors will cling to an investment, waiting for it to break even and get back to the price they paid for it. To avoid this happening, ask yourself: would I buy this investment again? And if you wouldn't, why are you continuing to own it? Another example is when investors focus too closely on their investment performance.

For example, if their portfolio has gone from £100,000 to £120,000 over the past year, they are happy. However, if during that twelve months their portfolio rose to £150,000 before dropping back to £120,000, they are upset. People mistakenly anchor to the high-water mark of their portfolios and are only satisfied when they hit an all-time high.

Framing

People's personality traits can hugely affect the way they react to the actual performance of their portfolio in the future. Consider a situation where two investors (Bob and Brian) have made the same investment. Over one year, the market average rises 10% but the individual investment value increases by 6%.

Bob cares only about the investment return and frames this as a gain of 6%. Brian is concerned with how the investment performs compared to the benchmark of the market average. The investment has lagged behind the market's performance and Brian frames this as a loss of 4%. Which investor is likely to be happier with the performance of their investment? Because individuals feel losses much more strongly than the pleasure of making a gain, Bob is much more likely to be happy with the investment than Brian.

Their differing reactions here will frame their future investment decisions. Another problem for investors is the strong tendency for individuals to frame their investments too narrowly – looking at performance over short time periods, even when their investment horizon is long-term. People also struggle to consider their portfolio as a whole, focusing too narrowly on the performance of individual components.

70% rule

Consider the 70% rule that advises people to plan on spending about 70% of their current income during their retirement. For most people, this rule of thumb is instantly appealing, which could explain why it has become so popular among financial planners.

Now let's reframe the 70% rule as the 30% rule and see what happens. That is, rather than focusing on the 70% of expenditure someone would keep through retirement, let's consider the 30% of expenditure that should be removed. Most people find the 30% rule difficult to digest, even though the 70% and 30% rules are mathematically identical.

Investors hate losses

According to Hersh Shefrin, people feel losses much more strongly than the pleasure of making a gain. This emotional strain is magnified when you assume responsibility for the loss. This guilt feeling then produces an avoidance to risk. But this level of guilt can be changed depending on how a financial decision is framed.

Myopic thinking

Do you focus too much attention on the short-term volatility of your portfolio? While it is not uncommon for an average stock or fund to change a few percentage points in a very short period of time, a myopic (i.e. shortsighted) investor may not react too favourably to the downside changes. This is a recipe for disaster if your goal is to achieve attractive returns over the long term.

Over-monitoring performance

How frequently you monitor your portfolio's performance can slant your understanding of it. Suppose you were investing over a 5 year period in higher risk funds.

Monitoring period		
Percentage of time seeing	5 year period	1-month period
Gains	90%	62%
Losses	10%	38%

Courtesy of ISACO.co.uk.

The table demonstrates how you would judge the portfolio depending on the monitoring period. Over the 5 year time frame, equity performance has been positive 90% of the time, and so risky investments do not lose money more than 10% of the time. However, if you were to monitor the performance of the same portfolio on a month-by-month basis, you would notice a loss 38% of the time![39]

Once again, because of our in-built dislike to loss, monitoring your portfolio more frequently will cause you to see more periods of loss, making you more likely to feel emotional stress and take less risk than is suitable for your long-term investment objectives.

Hindsight bias

Many events seem obvious in hindsight. Hindsight bias tends to occur in situations where a person believes (after the fact) that the beginning of some past event was predictable and completely obvious, whereas in fact, the event could not have been reasonably predicted. Psychologists connect hindsight bias to our inborn need to find order in the world by creating explanations that allow us to believe that events are predictable.

For example, many people now claim that signs of the technology bubble of the late 1990s and early 2000s (or any bubble in history, such as the Tulip bubble in the 1630s or the South Sea bubble of

1711) were obvious. This is a clear example of hindsight bias: if the creation of a bubble had been obvious at the time, it probably wouldn't have escalated and eventually burst.

Blame the adviser

Another example of hindsight bias is when an investor blames their adviser for choosing the worst performing fund in their portfolio. The investor suffering from hindsight bias will say things to their adviser like, 'Why did you recommend this underperforming fund?'

What the investor is unfortunately forgetting is that in a portfolio, there are always going to be winners and there are always going to be losers. The investor is failing to look at the bigger picture of the 'total performance' of their portfolio and see that it wasn't so obvious that the fund in question was going to turn out to be a poor performer.

Herd behaviour

One of the most shocking financial events in recent memory was the bursting of the internet bubble. However, this wasn't the first time that something like this had happened in the markets. But how could something so harmful be allowed to happen over and over again? The answer to this question can be found in what some people believe to be a hardwired human quality: herd behaviour, which is the tendency for individuals to copy the actions (rational or irrational) of a larger group.

Individually, however, most people would not necessarily make the same choice. While it's tempting to follow the newest investment trends, you are generally better off steering clear of the herd. Just because everyone is jumping on a certain investment bandwagon it doesn't necessarily mean that the strategy is correct.

Overconfidence

Another decision-making bias that humans are prone to is overconfidence (i.e. overestimating your ability to successfully perform a particular task). Psychological studies show that, although people differ in their levels of overconfidence, almost everyone displays it to some extent. For example, way more than half the population claim to be above average drivers, or have an above average sense of humour.

There is also an inclination for individuals to place too much confidence in their own investment decisions, beliefs and opinions. Lack of confidence is paralyzing, self-confidence is good, but overconfidence is deadly. Overconfidence can cause real problems for investors who mistake luck for skill. For instance, when something turns out well after a decision we've made, we claim the credit.

However, when something goes badly, we tend to see this as just bad luck. Many investors fall into the trap of believing that they can pick winning investments. As a result, they sometimes put too much of their wealth into one single investment, such as a company stock, which can be very risky. Research shows that picking winning investments is incredibly hard to do, even for professional investors.

Investors with too much confidence in their skills often buy and sell too frequently, which can have a negative effect on their returns. Overconfidence manifests itself when we think we can out-guess the market in terms of short-term movements, resulting in us trading actively, trying to capture each mini-peak-and-trough. Unfortunately, that usually just leaves active traders poorer.

A fine line between confidence and overconfidence

In a 2006 study entitled 'Behaving Badly', researcher James Montier found that 74% of the 300 professional fund managers surveyed believed that they had delivered above-average job performance. Of the remaining 26% surveyed, the majority viewed themselves as average. Incredibly, almost three quarters of the survey group believed that their job performance was average or better.

Clearly, only 50% of the sample can be above average, suggesting an insanely high level of overconfidence in the fund managers surveyed. As you can imagine, overconfidence is not a trait that applies only to fund managers. Keep in mind that there's a fine line between confidence and overconfidence. Confidence means realistically trusting in your own abilities, while overconfidence usually indicates an overly optimistic assessment of your knowledge or control of a situation.

How to avoid overconfidence

To avoid overconfidence in your own investing, I suggest you document and review your investment record. It's easy to remember your one stock that gained 50% in a single day, but records may reveal that most of your investments are under water for the year. Understanding the psychology that causes us to act overconfidently will help you avoid it.

Before we really understand something, we may either lack confidence or express overconfidence. A common type of overconfidence stems from inexperience. For instance, more than 70% of naive investors wrongly assume that they are enjoying above-average returns. Also bear in mind that professional fund managers, who have access to the best investment/industry reports and research in the business, can still struggle at achieving market-beating returns.

Human beings are not rational

As you've just discovered, psychological research has documented a range of biases that can affect decision making when it comes to money and investing. These biases sit deep within our psyche and, as fundamental parts of human nature, they affect all types of investors, both professional and private. Understanding them can help you to work around them.

Modern portfolio theory is built on the assumption of a rational being, who is unaffected by emotions such as greed, anxiety, regret, hope and fear. This super-rational investor simply does not exist. Everyone sees the world from a perspective which is uniquely theirs, and investing is no different. People have individual goals, requirements, desires, fears and hopes for their wealth.

What is your financial personality?

We all have different habits, different people we trust for advice, and different beliefs about the right decision on any occasion. But we all exhibit very similar psychological biases in our financial decision making, which can lead to poor portfolio choices and subpar investment performance.

Understanding your financial personality is vitally important. It can help you understand why you make the decisions you do, how you are likely to react to the deep-rooted uncertainty in investing, and how you can control the illogical elements of your investment decisions. In this chapter I've highlighted some of the psychological traps in investing that most people are susceptible to. Thinking about these in the light of your own financial personality will hopefully help you avoid them.

Okay, so now, my friend, we can move on to looking at how the professionals manage their portfolios. Would that be useful to you? Great, because in the next chapter you are going to discover the four questions you and every other investor need to ask on a daily basis. I'm also going to show you some extremely effective ways of dealing with market volatility and strategies for low and medium risk investors. I'll also give you some options for entering the market, how to make switches and ways you can add capital.

They say that unless you measure you can't manage, which is one reason we'll be looking at exactly how to measure investment success. I'm also going to give you some great tips on how to cope with temporary losses and provide you with you an excellent method to help preserve your ISA and SIPP wealth in volatile and falling markets.

I'll close off the next chapter by sharing with you a comprehensive list of the tools and resources that I personally use, and the good news is that many of them are free.

Let's go and discover…

10: How to Manage Your Portfolio

'The only way you get a real education in the market is to invest cash, track your trade, and study your mistakes!'
– Jesse Livermore

The rules are simple: If you manage your portfolio well, it will play a big part in helping you arrive at your financial goals on time. However, if you neglect your portfolio, your returns will probably suffer and that could result in taking longer than expected to reach your objectives. Let's begin this chapter by exploring what can happen to your retirement plans if you fail to achieve your target returns. In this example, I've used an investor with a £250,000 portfolio whose aim is to grow their investment account into a million pounds over the next twenty years.

To be successful, the investor's account would have to grow by 7.5% per year over the twenty year period – which I agree, is no easy feat. However, it is possible when you have all the correct components in place, such as knowing how to analyse the market's health, how to find good funds and knowing when to buy and when to exit.

How to double your money

The compounding rule is, when you achieve a 7.5% annual return, your money roughly doubles every 10 years. That means by achieving a return of 7.5% each year, £250,000 would turn into £500,000 over the course of the first 10 years, and the £500,000 would grow into £1 million in the final 10 years.

However, if you fail to get a reasonable return on your capital, it is going to take you much longer to reach your retirement goals. For example, if you achieved a 3.75% annual return, it would take you twice as long to get to your goal. Instead of reaching your objective in twenty years, it would take you forty!

Starting amount	Retirement goal	Annual growth rate	Time frame taken to hit retirement goal	Arrived at goal on time?
£250,000	£1 million	7.5%	20 years	Yes
£250,000	£1 million	3.75%	40 years	No, 20 years late.

Courtesy of ISACO.co.uk.

Your chief aim – beating the market

In **Chapter 6: How to Pick a Good Fund**, I said that when seeking long-term growth and higher returns for your ISA and SIPP, your main objective should be to beat the market. As you discovered, beating the market means doing better than a particular benchmark. You also discovered that it's not easy to do but possible.

Where people's opinions differ is when it comes to what benchmark they are measuring their performance against. In other words, which market, index, or indices they are trying to beat. As you've heard, our aim is to beat the NASDAQ Composite, arguably one of the strongest market indexes in the world. And with the NASDAQ being such a powerful index, it means it's a difficult task to beat it.

Even though we do try to beat the NASDAQ, our real goal is to outperform the FTSE 100. As you saw in earlier chapters, the FTSE 100 has not been as strong as the NASDAQ in the past, however it has annualised 4.8% since its inception 28 years ago[40]. That tells me that if we can beat the FTSE 100 over the long term, we're going to be blessed with a reasonable rate of return.

Our secret to beating the FTSE 100 by 60.2% over the last 16 years[41] (about 2.4% per year) is because we aim high. By aiming for the stars (to beat the NASDAQ) we end up getting to the moon (beating the FTSE 100). By doing the maths, if we continued to outperform the FTSE 100 at the same rate we have been, we might achieve a 7.2% return over a 28 year period, which would be an excellent long-term gain.

However, this last 16 years has been a sideways trending market and my belief is that we will be able to beat the FTSE 100 by more than 2.4% a year in better market conditions. For example, in the latest uptrend, which has so far lasted 5 years, we are proud to have beaten the FTSE 100 by 5.7% per year[42]. That shows you the possibilities of investing using my method if the market forms an uptrend over the next decade.

Four questions you have to ask yourself

My brother Paul and I were recently speaking to a DIY investor and found what he had to say extremely interesting. He told us about a time when he used a tip from a newspaper to pick a fund for his ISA and SIPP portfolio. The tip came from what the investor thought was a credible source and he explained that he was extremely pleased to receive a valuable recommendation at such a low price. However, the challenge came *after* buying it.

The investor was left feeling uncertain of what to do next. In the end, inertia got the better of him and he just left it alone, not really knowing whether he should keep it, sell it or switch into an alternative. This is not a good strategy. Burying your head in the sand after buying a fund and crossing your fingers and hoping for the best will not help you achieve a good rate of return. This situation is not uncommon. Many investors don't realise that there are four questions that need to be answered each and every day.

If you are unsure how to answer the questions, it's going to mean making decisions based on how you feel and this can result in poor investment choices. As you've discovered in earlier chapters, the stock market's character can change very quickly and unless you know how to effectively manage and monitor your portfolio, you could get into a spot of trouble.

The four questions you need to ask each and every day are:

1) Should I be invested right now?
2) If yes, should I be fully invested or partially invested?
3) If I should be invested, what should I be invested in?
4) Should I be staying in those investments or making an adjustment?

Question 1: Should I be invested right now?

If the market is in a bull phase, three out of four funds will move up and if the market is in a bear phase, three out of four funds are going to move down. Therefore, you don't really want to be invested in funds during bear markets, when most funds are falling.

Question 2: If yes, should I be fully invested or partially invested?

To answer this, you need to ask yourself, how strong is the uptrend? How's the market acting and behaving right now? How are leading stocks and leading funds acting? Where are we right now in the investment cycle? The key is to watch the market each and every day. It's also important to thoroughly analyse the market when it has closed and pay particular attention to the market's daily trading activity.

Question 3: If I should be invested, what should I be invested in?

This comes down to your objectives and risk profile. As you know, I'm an adventurous investor with an extremely long-term outlook and so my focus is always on investing in the highest quality funds and holding them over the long haul. As you discovered in **Chapter 6: How to Pick a Good Fund**, to find and buy a class fund, I use Morningstar.

Question 4: Should I be staying in those investments or making an adjustment?

This comes down to good management. Each day, you need to analyse the market and the funds you own and make a call if all is well. You will need to compare how your investments are doing by using a benchmark as your performance indicator. Ask the question, are my investments outperforming or underperforming my benchmark?

As you now know, the benchmarks we use are the NASDAQ Composite and the FTSE 100. When we see one of our funds underperform over an extended period, we know the institutional money has rotated out of the sector that the fund invests in. When this happens, we know that it's time to cut loose and find a better candidate. Remember that it's always best to be invested directly in the money flow.

Are you making decisions based on how you feel?

Do you feel confident about answering these four questions? Remember that you will need to ask and answer these questions each and every day throughout the year. Ask yourself, are you thoroughly analysing the market and your investments? Are you making the common mistake and making decisions based on how you feel? These days, many DIY investors choose their own investments, but soon after buying them they have no idea whether to remain fully invested, make a change, or to not be invested at all.

If they are invested, they become confused about whether they should still hold the investments or whether they should be making a switch. Unfortunately, most of them get caught up with the daily swings of the stock market. When emotions are running high and there is a general feeling of euphoria, they unfortunately buy at the top of the market. When markets are at their lows and there is a general feeling of despair and depression, they mistakenly sell.

Could you stomach a more volatile ride?

Your investment journey can be smooth or rocky depending on your aims and what you invest in. Here's a table that explains how your investment aims are connected to volatility, the quality of the ride.

Aim	Ride quality (Volatility)
High returns	Uncomfortable for risk averse investors
Medium returns	Fairly uncomfortable for risk averse investors
Low returns	Comfortable for risk averse investors

Courtesy of ISACO.co.uk.

We aim for high returns. That means the ride quality can be uncomfortable at times, especially for low to medium risk investors. The rule is: the higher the returns, the higher the risk and the higher the volatility.

Collective investments come with a risk rating, which can be found in the Key Investor Information Document (KIID) and is based on the historic weekly price changes of the fund over a 5 year period. Note that the fund company will use proxy data for recently launched funds. The categories on the scale correspond to different levels of volatility. The scale used is as follows:

Category	1	2	3	4	5	6	7
Annualised Volatility	Less than 0.5%	0.5–2%	2–5%	5–10%	10–15%	15–20%	More than 25%

Courtesy of ISACO.co.uk.

For example, funds in category 1 are normally cash based and have seen very little, or very gradual change in price over the last 5 years. Funds in category 6, into which the majority of equity-based funds fall, have seen more rapid changes in price over the last 5 years.

A simple way to lower volatility

If your aim is an annual return of 10–12%, it means you'll probably be purchasing funds with a risk rating of either 6 or 7. This means your portfolio in a typical year will experience price swings from its highs to its lows of up to 25% – or maybe even higher. If the threat of large temporary corrections in your account value doesn't appeal, and you'd be satisfied with a lower annual return in exchange for a smoother ride, I have a solution – you simply pair higher risk investments (adventurous funds) with lower risk investments (cash/fixed interest).

The most critical element of an investor's portfolio

Some of our clients do not share my adventurous nature. Many of them are either close to retirement or in retirement and are more concerned with protecting their wealth rather than aggressively growing it. Instead of aiming for 10–12% annual returns (like me), some are happy with between 3–5% per year and others are looking for an annual return in the region of 7–10%.

Some however, are adventurous like me and their ISA and SIPP portfolios will be made up purely of adventurous funds, which will be the same funds I'm personally invested in. However, our clients requiring a smoother ride in exchange for lower returns have portfolios that contain a combination of adventurous funds (the same ones I'm invested in), fixed interest and/or cash.

Whatever their return aims, I remind them that the most important part of their portfolio is the equity element (adventurous fund). This is because the equity is the tool you use to help generate your annual return. My take is that the fixed interest/cash portion of a portfolio serves one purpose only; to help reduce volatility.

The five key things to remember are:

1) Equity funds are what you use to help generate your annual return
2) Fixed interest and cash funds are your tools for lowering volatility
3) Use adventurous funds for the equity fund portion of your portfolio (risk rating 6 or 7)
4) Use Cash Parks and SIPP Bank Accounts for lowering volatility (risk rating 1)
5) If you prefer fixed interest over cash, use low risk rated (risk rating 2 or 3) quality bond funds

A perfect solution for low to medium risk ISA and SIPP investors

If you have a lower risk profile than me and/or a shorter investment horizon, my suggestion would be to use high quality adventurous funds for the equity element (which might be 50%) when creating your portfolio. For the fixed interest/cash portion of your portfolio (the other 50%), my number one preference would be the ISA Cash Park and/or a SIPP Bank Account, which both carry a risk rating of 1.

These are both perfect to be used in combination with adventurous funds. However, take note that the ISA Cash Park can only be used as a temporary solution because HMRC do not like you keeping your capital in the Cash Park over long periods. If you have a SIPP, I suggest you use a SIPP Bank Account. If a client preferred to use fixed interest instead of cash as their tool for lowering the volatility, I would suggest they look for a quality bond fund.

A fixed interest fund we like: The M&G Short Dated Corporate Bond A

The fixed interest fund we used to tell our clients about was the Fidelity Moneybuilder Income Fund A-Income-Gross (ISIN: GB0032346800). In the 2003–2007 bull market, the MoneyBuilder Income Fund carried a risk rating of 2 but right now it carries a risk rating of 4, which means its risk rating and its volatility have significantly increased over the last five years.

One fund that we prefer right now is the M&G Short Dated Corporate Bond A (ISIN: GB0031110397), which comes with a risk rating of 3. A score of 3 means that over the last 5 years its annual volatility has been between 2% and 5%, which is very low. Some investors mistakenly think that all bond funds are safe and low risk.

However this is far from the truth and at the time of writing, there are many bond funds that carry risk ratings of 5 out of a possible 7 – and that means their annual volatility over the last five years has been between 10% and 15%. A risk rating of 5 means the fund has been behaving more like an equity fund. Pairing up adventurous funds with fixed interest funds that carry high risk ratings – such as 4 or 5 – is not the best strategy for helping you to lower volatility.

Just remember that your best tool for reducing volatility is cash. Always bear in mind that the equity portion of your portfolio is the most important element – because it's the part that helps you get your return – and the tools to use to lower your volatility need to carry very low risk ratings and ideally a risk rating of 1. And if you are an investor who prefers fixed interest funds over cash, aim to use a bond fund that carries a risk rating of 3 or below.

How much risk are you willing to take?

When constructing your portfolio, you could consider one of these five different models: Defensive, Cautious, Balanced, Growth or Aggressive. These are shown just as a guide to give you an idea of how your portfolio could be made up.

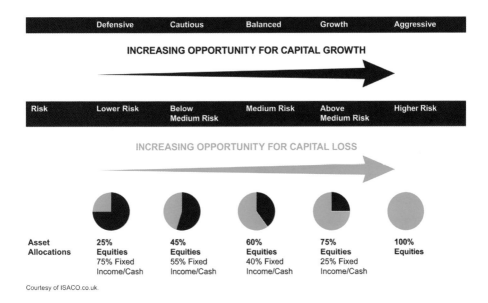

Courtesy of ISACO.co.uk.

As you can see, the level of risk to your capital increases as you progress through the investment model spectrum. In addition, the potential for capital growth over the investment time horizon increases along the investment model spectrum. The selected model will govern your asset allocation and in all instances, I suggest that exposure to equities can be achieved by way of collective funds.

Now that we've covered how to lower volatility and construct a portfolio to suit your requirements, let's move on to some tips and hints for professionally managing your portfolio.

A way to keep it simple

We like to keep things simple. We talk to lots of investors who own far too many investment funds – sometimes as many as 70 or even more! We normally buy about five or six funds and our maximum would probably be no more than eight.

The problem is that if you own too many investments, you can't watch them all closely enough. That means monitoring and managing them becomes a challenge. Sometimes, we find that people over diversify, which can often be a hedge for ignorance. If you over diversify, it will eat into your returns and you'll struggle to beat the market.

How to manage your account: making a switch

Let's look at how switching works and review the three rules.

Rule 1 – In bull markets (uptrend) invest into funds
Rule 2 – If your fund underperforms, switch into another fund
Rule 3 – In bear markets (downtrend) park in cash

Market cycles are continuous. After the bull market is over, the bear market begins. When we believe a new bear market has begun, we switch into cash and stay in cash until we believe the bear market is over. The cycle of bull market followed by bear market continues forever.

Three types of possible switches

Whilst investing, you will encounter three types of possible switch scenarios.

1) Switching from a fund into an alternative fund.
2) Switching from a fund into the ISA Cash Park/SIPP Bank Account.
3) Switching from the ISA Cash Park/SIPP Bank Account into a fund.

1) Switching from a fund into an alternative fund

The first type of switch occurs only during bull markets. This type of switch takes place when you are invested in a fund that you believe is underperforming. When this happens, you have the option of making a switch from the underperforming fund into an alternative fund.

For example:
- The market is in a bull phase
- You own 4 funds: Fund A, Fund B, Fund C and Fund D
- You have a 25% allocation in each fund

- You are 100% fully invested
- Fund D is underperforming
- You make a switch out of Fund D into Fund X
- After the transaction is complete, you own Fund A, B, C and X
- You have a 25% allocation in each fund

2) Switching from a fund into the ISA Cash Park/SIPP Bank Account

This second type of switch occurs when you believe the market has changed from bull to bear. This type of switch will take place when you are invested in funds and believe the market has changed its major trend from up to down. When this happens, you have the opportunity to make a switch from the funds you own into the ISA Cash Park/SIPP Bank Account.

For example:

- The market is in a bull phase
- You own 4 funds: Fund A, Fund B, Fund C and Fund D
- You have a 25% allocation in each fund
- You are 100% fully invested
- A new bear market begins/a major downtrend is triggered
- You make a switch out of Funds A, B, C and D into the ISA Cash Park/SIPP Bank Account
- After the transaction is complete, you are 100% invested in the ISA Cash Park/SIPP Bank Account

3) Switching from the ISA Cash Park/SIPP Bank Account into a fund

This third type of switch occurs when you believe a new bull market has begun. This takes place after a bear market is over and, if you got your timing right, you will be parked in the ISA Cash Park/SIPP Bank Account. When you believe a new bull market has started, you switch from the ISA Cash Park/SIPP Bank Account into a fund.

For example:

- The market is in a bear phase
- You are 100% invested in the ISA Cash Park/SIPP Bank Account
- A new bull market begins
- You make a switch out of the ISA Cash Park/SIPP Bank Account into Funds E, F, G and H
- You allocate 25% to each fund
- After the transaction is complete, you are 100% invested
- After the transaction is complete, you own Funds E, F, G and H

Keeping your switches to a minimum is a smart move

As you've heard in previous chapters, we normally make no more than four switches in a year. As soon as we believe the new bull market has started, we switch into high quality funds. We then remain invested all the way through the bull market and will only switch into an alternative fund if our fund or funds are underperforming. We also remain fully invested in funds during bull market corrections. Bull market correction periods can be anything from 8–25% in depth.

Two ways to add capital

You can add capital as a lump sum or alternatively, you can drip feed it in using a pound cost averaging strategy. If you are a long-term investor, you can also add capital at the same time each and every year, such as the start or end of the tax year. For almost every single year of the 16 years that I've been investing in ISAs, I've added the full ISA allowance in the first one or two weeks of the new tax year.

This means that by April 20th each and every year, my ISA allowance has normally been invested. If I was invested in funds at this time, I'd simply allocate the new capital into the funds I was currently invested in. If I was parked in cash, I'd wait for the signal from the market to give me the green light to invest.

Boosting your returns by strategic buying on dips

Another thing to consider (if you are a long-term investor) when adding capital is strategic buying on dips, which could also boost your returns. To make this work, you need to buy into the theory that markets always go higher. Your buy on the dips rule might be something along the lines of, 'when the market is 10% off its high, you add capital'.

Or it might be, 'when the market is 20% off its high, you add capital'. It doesn't have to be perfect, as long as you are adding when the market isn't trading at its highs. This is a simple but highly effective strategy, however it takes courage to pull it off because when the market is in a correction, you normally do not feel like buying and feel more like selling.

How do you measure success?

There is a psychological game being played by the financial services industry with unsuspecting investors. In general, IFAs, fund supermarkets, wealth managers, banks and stocks brokers don't tell their investor clients how important it is to measure their annual performance. They know that typically, DIY investors forget their losers and focus on their winners. Due to overconfidence, something you learned about in the previous chapter, many investors tend to kid themselves into thinking they are doing much better than they are in reality.

The result unfortunately, is that most market participants underperform the general market. If the advice industry told their clients to measure their annual performance against a benchmark such as the FTSE 100, they'd end up losing a lot of business. Why? Simply because people using their services would eventually realise that what they were being sold may sound good in theory but in reality, doesn't work.

How many IFAs do you know who tell their clients how they've performed for them and whether their performance has beaten the market? The answer is probably not that many. When you visit fund supermarket sites, how many of them tell you to measure your performance? I don't know one that does and once again, it's because they have to protect their business models.

If you seek growth, this is what you need to do

As I said in this book's introduction, the investment advice industry is failing miserably in helping investors achieve their financial objectives. If you are seeking growth, my suggestion would be to try to beat the NASDAQ and the FTSE 100 over the long term. This means that the NASDAQ Composite and the FTSE 100 would be your benchmarks. Each year, make a note of the price that both these indexes are trading at, as well as noting your ISA and SIPP account value.

Also, make a note of any additional capital injections, such as annual ISA additions and document any withdrawals you make. At the end of each year, look at what the NASDAQ and the FTSE 100 are trading at and how much your account is valued at. Next, calculate the percentage change of the FTSE 100 for the year. If your account has grown by a larger percentage than the FTSE 100, it is classed as a success. And if it's outperformed the NASDAQ Composite, it's classed as an even greater success.

The idea is to keep a track of your annual performance as you move through time. Do this regardless of whether you are getting help or not. It's important that you know how well or how badly you are doing so that you can either keep on doing what's working, or change your approach – or adviser – because it isn't working.

How to deal with temporary losses

If you decide to invest in funds linked to the stock market, you must prepare yourself for temporary losses. The market does not go up in a straight line and must correct in price from time to time. Sometimes bull market corrections can be quite scary and they hurt. If you make the mistake of checking your account value each day, the short-term sharp drops could make you feel physically sick.

Corrections over the latest bull market have been varied in length and size and the largest one was 22.9% in depth, which began in the spring of 2011. My belief is that you can only win in the long term if you accept volatility, risk and temporary losses in the shorter term.

A great tip for coping with drops in your investment account

Here's a nice tip I learned. If your losses ever cause you to lose sleep, it means you are probably investing too much money and need to scale down. A good idea might be to switch some of your capital out of the market. Also remember that your investing does not need to be an all or nothing decision. When you begin, you can invest say, 50% and leave the other 50% in cash.

Let's now look at how you would feel if you were to take a big percentage drop on your portfolio. This of course would be what we call a temporary or paper loss. If you are playing the long-term game, the loss should be viewed as a temporary setback. This means that you may have to be temporarily inconvenienced for some time, especially during bear markets. Let's look at how this works.

Imagine that you invested £100 into the stock market. Then the market and your fund heads south over the next twelve months. The net result is your £100 dropping to £70, a 30% drop. How would you feel about that 30% loss? Sitting on a paper loss of £30 may not seem too much of an inconvenience but what if the amount invested was more? What if your portfolio was valued at £250,000?

In this case, sitting temporarily on a paper loss of £75,000 would cause some people tremendous stress and anxiety. On the other hand, people with the right mindset would be more comfortable. Imagine taking a temporary 30% loss on one million pounds. Can you imagine taking a £300,000 temporary paper loss? What's important to understand is that throughout your investing career, you are going to have ugly short-term periods in the market and you need to start preparing now for how you are going to deal with it when it happens.

Winning investors cope with paper losses by thinking long-term and expect ups and downs throughout their investing term. When an adventurous investor aims for double digit gains over the long term, they learn how to deal with temporary losses and see them as nothing more than a short-term set back.

How to preserve ISA and SIPP wealth

You've learned that the ideal aim for the ISA and SIPP investor is to profit in bull markets and protect in bear markets. You've also discovered that bull markets can be seen as the boom part of the stock market cycle and bear markets can be seen as the bust part. Take a look at this table, which will remind you of my approach to investing.

Market description	Type of market	Estimated length of time	Aim	Frequent trading?
Bull market.	Rising.	2–4 years.	Profit – Invest in high quality investment funds.	No, 4 trades or less per year.
Bear market.	Falling.	9–18 months.	Protect – Use a Cash Park/SIPP Bank Account to preserve profits.	No, stay parked in cash for 9–18 months.

Courtesy of ISACO.co.uk.

Fidelity's ISA Cash Park

You've heard a lot about the ISA Cash Park. You can use the Cash Park to protect your portfolio in bear markets and you can also use it for the times when you have money ready to invest but need more time to pick your funds. ISA Cash Parks are a temporary shelter for your ISA allowance. In an ISA Cash Park, your investment is held as cash and earns interest.

SIPP investors who wish to de-risk their portfolio can move money into a SIPP Bank Account. While cash can be held over the long term in your SIPP, you can only hold cash temporarily within a stocks and shares ISA. The key here is that this must only be a temporary move and you should intend to reinvest the money at some point.

Tools and resources for the smart DIY investor

I thought I'd end this chapter by sharing some of the tools and resources my team, our clients and I use to help us make better informed investment decisions:

Investors.com (http://www.investors.com/default.htm)

I like Investors.com a lot. There's loads of free stuff but some of their better content is subscription only. In the subscription only section, they run a daily column called 'The Big Picture', which gives you their take on the market. They put their neck on the line by telling you whether they believe the market is in a confirmed rally (green light to invest) or whether the market is in a correction phase (park in cash).

The column is useful just to get a second opinion after you've conducted your daily market analysis. Investors.com is part of *Investor's Business Daily* (IBD), a national newspaper in the United States. Founded in 1984 by William O'Neil, its headquarters are in Los Angeles, California.

IBD provides detailed information about US stocks, mutual funds, commodities, and other financial instruments aimed at individual investors. The Investors.com website provides detailed, concise statistics using earnings, stock price performance, and other criteria to help investors find quality stocks. The information is designed to be used along with William O'Neil's book *How to Make Money in Stocks*. My views on how the markets work syncs up with IBD's perfectly.

MarketSmith (http://www.marketsmith.com/)

MarketSmith is a wholly owned company of William O'Neil + Company and an affiliate of Investor's Business Daily. It is a US based service and the stocks in its database trade mainly on the US markets rather the UK markets. It's my personal investment research tool and I love it.

It provides institutional-quality data and allows you to gain access to the same high-quality data used by professional portfolio managers. You could say it's your one-stop destination for superior investment research. You can search for the best performing stocks and quickly analyse the market indexes. The site allows you to access stock charts with a great blend of technical and fundamental data. The research package comes at a cost ($999 US per year) but you can opt for a trial before you buy.

Morningstar.co.uk (http://www.morningstar.co.uk/)

What a wonderful site this is. We've been using Morningstar since it started and we couldn't have outperformed the market without their help. We use the site to search for funds throughout the year and we also use it to help us time our buys. It's easy to set up multiple portfolios (for free) and get daily alerts sent directly to your inbox telling you how your portfolio is performing.

Morningstar UK opened in London in 2000 and launched its individual investor website in 2001. In 2013 Morningstar was voted a 'Top Website to Save You Money' by *The Times*. The website offers access to and objective information on more than 9,000 funds available to individual investors in the UK and 42,000 stocks worldwide.

The site offers educational guidance and independent editorial content, produced by Morningstar analysts and journalists based in London and around the world. I'm proud of the fact that Holly Cook, Managing Editor of Morningstar.co.uk, is a friend of mine.

Fidelity (https://www.fidelity.co.uk/)

I've been a client of Fidelity since 1997 and a user of their FundsNetwork investment platform since it began its operation back in 2000. Personally, I not only use the site to track my ISA and SIPP investment portfolio, I also use it for gathering information relating to investing. They also have some really good free guides and reports.

MoneyWeek (http://www.moneyweek.com/)

MoneyWeek is a great free resource to tap into. I have read many articles on their site and all of them have been interesting, informative and extremely well written. Many of our high net worth clients love MoneyWeek and I am yet to hear a bad word about them.

What Investment (http://www.whatinvestment.co.uk/)

I have read many great articles on *What* Investment. I especially like the content written by the editor, Nick Britton.

Investment Week (http://www.investmentweek.co.uk/)

Time and time again the Google News Alerts service picks up great articles from Investment Week's website. Investment Week provides great content and coverage of the investment market and the site's content is written by a team that has a vast wealth of market knowledge.

Jim Paulson (https://www.wellscap.com/index.html)

Jim Paulsen is an optimist, a long-term bull (like me) and always seems to offer great market insights. Jim is the Chief Investment Strategist at Wells Capital Management. Jim is nationally recognised for his views on the economy. He frequently appears on CNBC and Bloomberg Television programs, including regular appearances as a guest host on CNBC.

BusinessWeek named him Top Economic Forecaster and *BondWeek* twice named him Interest Rate Forecaster of the Year. His newsletter 'Economic and Market Perspective', was named one of '101 Things Every Investor Should Know' by *Money* magazine. You can sign up for free to his newsletter, which I always feel is great value.

Bob Doll (http://www.nuveen.com/Commentary/BobDoll/Weekly Commentary.aspx)

Bob Doll is Nuveen Asset Management's Chief Equity Strategist and Senior Portfolio Manager. Bob provides a superb 'Weekly Investment Commentary' that I also highly recommend. It's free and packed with great thoughts and key investment-related information.

Jeremy Siegel (http://www.jeremysiegel.com/)

Jeremy Siegel is one of those guys you find hard not to like and he always seems to be smiling. Like Jim Paulson, he's a long-term bull and an eternal optimist. Jeremy is the Professor of Finance at the Wharton School, University of Pennsylvania. Siegel comments on the economy and financial markets: he appears regularly on networks such CNN and CNBC, and writes regular columns for *Kiplinger's Personal Finance* and Yahoo! Finance. Jeremy has written two books, *Stocks for the Long Run* and *The Future for Investors*.

CNBC (TV and App) (http://www.cnbc.com/)

CNBC is a great TV channel and does have some fantastic guests. I also have the CNBC app on my Ipad and Iphone. The app is free and it's awesome. It allows you to quickly set up a portfolio of stocks. One thing I like to do is keep a close eye on the stocks that form part of the portfolios of funds I own.

Yahoo! Finance (http://uk.finance.yahoo.com/)

I use Yahoo! Finance for keeping an eye on the various exchanges around the world. If I ever buy funds that invest in UK companies, I set up a portfolio for free on Yahoo! Finance (because MarketSmith does not cover UK stocks) and that helps me track the top ten holdings of the UK funds I own.

Monevator (http://monevator.com/)

The UK has a serious shortage of good investment blogs. One blog that's a real gem is called Monevator.

Books

Books are a great resource, especially when they are written by real life investors who have proven track records.

Here are 14 I strongly recommend:

How to Make Money in Stocks – William O'Neil
24 Essential Lessons for Investment Success – William O'Neil
The Successful Investor – William O'Neil
My Own Story – Bernard Baruch
The Battle for Investment Survival – Gerald Loeb
How to Trade in Stocks – Jesse Livermore
How I Made $2,000,000 in the Stock Market – Nicolas Darvas
One Up On Wall Street – Peter Lynch
Market Wizards – Jack Schwager
The New Market Wizards – Jack Schwager
Reminiscences of a Stock Operator – Edwin Lefevre
Big Money Little Effort – Mark Shipman
The Next Big Investment Boom – Mark Shipman
Trader Vic – Victor Sperandeo

Okay, now it's time to move on my friend.

But before we do that, let me ask you a couple of questions.

Do you desire an income for life?

Is your aim a secure and richer retirement?

If you answered yes to these questions, then the next chapter is for you. It's crammed with information but one thing I think you are going to love is my 5 step plan for creating a lifetime income. In this next chapter I'm also going to tell you why 'lifestyling' is flawed and totally outdated.

And I'll show you a great strategy I'm currently executing on behalf of my dad, who is looking to invest a significant amount of capital into the market over the next five years. This 'passive' strategy is designed for people who want to leave a legacy. It's something I highly recommend. I'm certain that you'll be excited when you discover that it's a perfect solution for leaving your mark and an excellent way to achieve a 7–10% annual return on capital outside your ISA and SIPP.

Excited?

Good. Let's take at look together at how you'd go about…

11: Creating an Income for Life

'Few people take objectives really seriously. They put average effort into too many things, rather than superior thought and effort into a few important things. People who achieve the most are selective as well as determined.'
– Richard Koch

Imagine sitting down on the day of your retirement to plan your financial future. You know what your annual expenses have been and you want to maintain your current standard of living. So, you consult a recent mortality table and find that if you've made it to your 65th birthday, you can expect to live to 85 years old.

You perform a little calculation and find that, together with your State Pension entitlements, you have just enough savings to maintain your current standard of living and spend all of your savings and future expected earnings by the time you die at the age of 85. But, what if you live longer? Will you be reduced to scraping out an existence on State Pension entitlements alone?

The risk of retirees outliving their retirement savings

Many people today are discussing the 'retirement crisis', noting that individuals do not save enough and will not accumulate enough cash to retire comfortably. But there is another approaching crisis that is quickly attracting attention: post-retirement. While the retirement crisis centres on the financial struggles of people saving for retirement, the post-retirement crisis focuses on the financial difficulties of people near or in retirement.

To illustrate the unique financial complexities facing retirees, consider 10 school friends who decide to retire at age 65. Now guess when the first of these friends will die. As it turns out, the first death is likely to occur only 8 years into retirement at age 73. Next, try guessing when the last person will die.

The answer is 36 years into retirement, at age 101[43]. Put differently, one retiree needs to pay for just 8 years of expenses, whereas another has to pay for 36 years of expenses. Therefore, the risk of retirees outliving their retirement savings is significant. You could also argue that this longevity risk is actually far greater than investment risk.

A mistake made by investors

Many investors in their late 50s and 60s – approaching retirement or already in – have been coached by media and industry professionals to think about their investing time horizons in a way that, in my view is all wrong. Most people naturally think their time horizon ends when they retire, or when they stop contributing to their retirement funds, or when they start taking cash regularly from their portfolio. They mistakenly think that's when they should reduce most, if not all volatility risk and start thinking ultra conservatively.

Why thinking ultra conservatively could be dangerous

Thinking ultra conservatively can frequently mean an unnecessary and sometimes serious reduction in quality of life later on. Why? People live longer than ever now, yet many invest, by and large, like they expect to die at age 70. Thanks to better education, nutrition and technological and medical innovations, people are living longer today than thought leaders were predicting 50 years ago.

According to the Office of National Statistics, based on 2008–10 mortality rates, a man aged 65 could expect to live another 17.8 years, and a woman aged 65 another 20.4 years. That means the average 65 year old male will live until they are 83 but some 65 year old men will beat this average and live even longer. And my guess is, much longer.

My suggestion is...

In these next 20 years, there are going to be more medical advancements than we can fully comprehend now and today's retiree is overall more fit, active and healthy than ever before. If you're 65 years old or approaching 65, my suggestion is to adopt a long-time investment horizon, especially if you come from a long-living family and are in good health.

Many investors approaching their retirement mistakenly think that reducing risk by moving out of equities and into bonds and cash instruments is smart. It's true that having a portfolio of gilts and cash won't be as volatile, but volatility risk is just one kind of risk.

There's investment risk – the risk that your bonds don't perform. There's also opportunity risk – the risk of missing out on a better investment.

Running out of money, a fear worse than death

In a 2010 poll conducted by Allianz Life Insurance Co of North America on people aged 44 to 75, more than 3 in 5 (61%) said that they feared depleting their assets more than they feared dying. By thinking too short term, many investors approaching retirement invest too conservatively, resulting in poor returns, failing to stay ahead of inflation and, as the years pass by, their retirement pot slowly but surely becomes smaller and smaller.

When approaching your retirement, please don't make the fatal mistake of failing to plan for a long enough time horizon. Volatility and sitting through market corrections may make the investor feel bad in the near term, but if they die before their spouse and fail to plan for the correct time horizon, they could be leaving their partner in aged poverty.

Personally, I think it's a big gamble to assume that you and your spouse will be just average and live another 10 years – because you could find out that you're abnormally healthy, live another 20 or 30 years and run out of money after 10. Plus, it's later in life that you'll probably want the additional comforts money can buy. Therefore, investing too conservatively could be seen as high risk.

Without risk, you can't get growth

If you have a long time to invest and most likely you do, the odds are in your favour. The longer your time horizon, the greater the odds that equities will treat you better than cash or bonds – and by a wide margin. Most investors with a long time horizon – 20 years or more – likely need at least some growth. And let's not forget about inflation's impact, which historically is running at about 3% per year, and the cost of investing, roughly 1–3% per year.

Retirees who need their investment portfolios to beat the pace of inflation, the cost of investing and provide some cash flow are doing themselves a disservice by removing all or even most volatility risk from their portfolios.

Without risk, you can't get growth. And without growth, a portfolio can be ravaged over time by withdrawals, the cost of investing and inflation. To help a portfolio survive the long haul, you likely need to hold some portion of your portfolio in stocks most of the time. And as you've seen in previous chapters, you can lower the risk of buying individual shares, and provide better diversification, by buying quality funds and holding them over the long term.

How to create a lifetime income

If you buy into my thinking that investing too conservatively could be seen as being risky, you'll probably agree with my 5 step plan for creating a lifetime income:

1) Switch to long-term thinking

2) Invest for growth
3) Health and wellness
4) Time and compound interest
5) Smart income drawdown

1) Switch to long-term thinking

As you've just discovered, many unsuspecting investors make the fatal mistake, when approaching retirement, of failing to plan for a long enough time horizon. Now knowing that many people will live 20–30 years after hitting retirement, you may have realised that you have been thinking too short-term. If so, you now have the opportunity to rethink your plan.

2) Invest for growth

By extending your investment time horizon, you have the opportunity to take on more risk. One option would be to invest in slightly more adventurous funds; funds that have the potential for attractive long-term returns.

And as you've discovered, smart investors use tax wrappers such as ISAs and SIPPs to further boost their returns and pay less tax. Outperforming the market over the long term may be extremely difficult to achieve but it is possible. When you're successful in beating the market, it helps you achieve higher returns; helping to reduce the risk of running out of capital later in life.

3) Health and wellness

When an investor changes from short-term thinking to long-term thinking and decides that they are going to aim for growth by investing in growth-oriented funds, another area they ought to consider is their health and wellbeing.

Scientists refer to the following determinants of longevity: country of residence, the country's health care system, genetics, standard of living, healthy behaviour, education and environment. Even though some things are out of our control, such as our genetics, each of us has the power to choose – allowing us the potential to make better decisions relating to our health and wellbeing.

Each of us can decide to take better care of ourselves by learning more about health and nutrition, eating the right foods, exercising regularly and resting appropriately. On the other hand, we can decide to stay ignorant about health and nutrition, eat the wrong foods, refrain from exercise and generally neglect our bodies. The choice is always our own. One course of action will help, and the other will hurt. If you are like me, you already buy into the healthy living concept.

4) Time and compound interest

In **Chapter 2: ISAs – Aiming to become an ISA Millionaire**, you saw the incredible effect compounding has on money when invested over the long term, especially when you can get your money to grow at a decent rate of return. When you set a longer time horizon and are successful at achieving higher returns, the result is an increased chance of arriving at your financial objectives. It also lessens the probability of running out of money during your retirement.

5) Smart income drawdown

Creating a lifetime income is possible if you take the appropriate action to increase your chances of success. When reaching a long-term target, which could be anything from £500,000 to £15 million or even more, a smart investor could set up an automatic withdrawal plan from their ISA and SIPP accounts to pay them the income to fund their lifestyle.

The guideline rule is to take out a smaller percentage rate than the rate your account is growing at. If an investor had been making 8% per year over the long term, the guiding rule would be to withdraw maybe 3% or 4% each year, ensuring that their retirement pot would continue to grow. If they continued to stick with this simple formula, they would be in effect eliminating the risk of running out of capital and at the same time, creating a continuous stream of lifetime income.

Why 'lifestyling' is a flawed strategy

Lifestyling is the practice of reducing the risk to a pension or other investment, typically by shifting to less volatile and lower risk investments. If a fund uses lifestyling, the assets are moved out of equities and into safer investments, such as government bonds and cash, as the investor approaches retirement.

Sometimes these types of funds are called 'target funds'. I believe lifestyling is a flawed strategy – a concept that's totally outdated. 30 or 40 years ago, when people weren't living as long as they are now, the idea of lifestyling may have been a good way to think about investing. However today, a healthy 65 year-old is looking at a life expectancy of 83. That's eighteen more years of spending and eighteen more years of inflation to erode the buying power of his or her money!

The 4 skills of the master investor

My thinking is that you have to aim high and make decisions based upon you living much longer than you may have previously thought. As you now know, inflation chips away at the buying power of money, and fees and charges associated with investing can also quickly add up. The key is to condition yourself to think differently. You need to aim high and try to master these four skills:

Skill 1 – How to find and invest in funds likely to beat the market
Skill 2 – How to time your buys and exits with greater accuracy
Skill 3 – How to get in sync with the market and trade with the trend instead of against it
Skill 4 – How to keep all associated costs, charges and fees low

The good news is that I have shared my skills in these areas with you and so all you now need to do is go out there and practice, practice, practice. By mastering these four key disciplines, you'll have a much better chance of achieving your aims. And if you feel you don't have time, get help from a trusted professional you admire and respect.

How to increase the likelihood of staying ahead of the market

The key is to think long-term. See losses in corrections as temporary inconveniences and refrain from getting spooked out of the market in volatile and challenging environments. When you get all these elements right, you'll increase the likelihood of staying ahead of the market and achieving a reasonable rate of return on your capital.

When you make better informed investment decisions, you increase the probability of making a return that outpaces both inflation and the costs associated with investing. Trying to achieve higher returns is going to take time to master. It will involve a tremendous amount of willpower, plenty of hard work and, it goes without saying, a little bit of luck.

Think of your wealth like a cake

I like to think of your total wealth like a cake, split into thirds. I believe that when you reach retirement, which might be at 55 for some, 65 for others and 75 for those who love their work, I suggest that one third of your wealth is invested in the stock market, another third is invested in property and the final third invested in your own business or businesses. Think multiple streams of income.

The stock market and the property market work in cycles. Both of them have bull and bear markets, which means that sometimes they'll be in an uptrend, sometimes a downtrend and sometimes there will be periods where they won't make any price progress for many years. However, if you look at the stock and property markets over the last century, they are both in long-term uptrends.

This means that sometimes the stock market will be hot and other times the property market will be having a nice run. Sometimes your business or businesses will be flourishing. My expertise is not in knowing how to build a property portfolio and neither does it lie in building a business empire. However, I can give you some pointers regarding the third of your wealth that I believe should be invested in the stock market.

Profit from combining an active strategy with a passive strategy

With the third of your wealth that you allocate to investing in the stock market, I suggest you consider two strategies. The first is an active strategy and the second is more passive. The active strategy involves using your ISAs and SIPP to invest in adventurous funds over the long term. This is your tax sheltered strategy, when you buy quality funds at the lowest possible cost and aim to beat the market.

For money outside an ISA and SIPP, I don't recommend this active strategy because the capital gains tax (CGT) that you'll have to pay will eat into your returns and probably result in underperforming the market. Your passive strategy is one where you don't buy and exit like I suggest you do with your ISA and SIPP strategy. With this passive approach, you'll only be buying, which means there will be no CGT to pay until much further down the road when you start taking income.

By putting in and not taking out, you completely avoid paying CGT, which means you'll benefit from the incredible power of compounding. This passive strategy is a simple one that involves investing in a low cost index fund or ETF that tracks the S&P 500, and staying fully invested in the fund over the long term. It's a strategy that I'm currently executing on behalf of my dad, who is looking to invest a significant amount of capital into the market over the next five years. We call this our 'S&P 500 Strategy'.

How to leave a legacy: the S&P 500 Strategy

If you want to invest in something that you can benefit from yourself, and leave for others to benefit from after you're gone, this could be the strategy for you. The idea is that you will be investing in the S&P 500 for an infinite amount of time, which means the fund will outlive you. Whilst you're alive, it will provide income for you to enjoy and once you're gone, it will continue to provide income for future generations of your family, or alternatively, a charity or cause close to your heart.

The goal of this strategy is to mirror the performance of the S&P 500. By purchasing a fund such as the HSBC American Index Fund (ISIN:GB00B80QG615), you're buying the S&P 500 Index. Purchasing this fund is one way to mirror the performance of the S&P 500 but it's not the only way. There is an ETF (Ticker symbol: SPY) you could use and there are lots of other funds that also aim to track the performance of the S&P 500.

When searching for a suitable tracker, the three things to really keep your eye on are the total expense ratio (TER), the fund's liquidity and its tracking error. We like to buy trackers at low cost, we like them to be liquid and we like them to have minimal tracking error. If they have a low TER, the tracking error is also usually low. For example, the HSBC American Index Fund has a TER (ongoing charge) of just 0.18% and this tells me the tracking error will be minute.

The returns you can make using this strategy cannot be ignored. During the ten years ending on December 31st 2012, the S&P 500 registered an average annual total return of 7.09%. This return was made during an abnormally weak period. I believe that over the long term, mirroring the S&P 500 would probably net you a return of approximately 7–10% per year. This would allow whoever was going to benefit from the fund to draw an income of say, 2–3% per year, allowing the fund to continue to grow at a decent annual rate of return.

S&P 500 Strategy

This method is very simple and consists of four easy steps.

Step 1 – Decide the total amount to invest
For example: £1,000,000.

Step 2 – Decide the time frame for your buy program
For example: Buy program evenly spread over 5 years.

Step 3 – Decide on the number of purchases
For example: 5 equal purchases of £200,000.

Step 4 – Decide when the purchases will take place

For example: On January 1ˢᵗ, for the next five years, buy £200,000 of the HSBC American Index Fund.

Once all your purchases are done, you can sit back and simply let your investment grow. However, there are some clever tactics you can use to help give the fund a boost, which I'm going to share with you in a moment.

How would you feel if…

Losses may occur over the short term and, as you discovered in **Chapter 10: How to Manage Your Portfolio**, the way to deal with these losses is to think long term and see them as temporary.

During your five year buy program, you are likely to experience at least one bear market and during the bear market, you may feel like cashing in and aborting the whole program. A bear market could surface as soon as your program starts and that means your first buy falling as much as 20% or even much more. How would you feel about that? How would you feel about adding the same amount you added in year one when you are already down 20% or more? These are questions that need careful thought before proceeding.

Smart tactics for boosting your returns: Bear market strategy

As an additional strategy, if you are willing to be more aggressive and want to capitalise on buying the market when it is cheap, you could adopt a bear market strategy to supplement your long-term pound cost averaging strategy. With this approach, you aim to buy when the market is low by purchasing three equal amounts in the trough of the bear market. The first buy is when the S&P 500 is 20% off its recent high, the second buy is three months later and the final buy three months after that.

How does the S&P 500 bear market strategy work?

The strategy consists of 5 simple steps.

Step 1 – You decide on an amount you want to invest

Step 2 – You divide that amount by three

Step 3 – Purchase number one occurs when the S&P 500 is 20% off its high

Step 4 – Purchase number two is scheduled for three months later

Step 5 – Purchase number three occurs three months after purchase number two

Further opportunities to buy when the market is low

Every three months after the third purchase, if the market is trading *lower* than the third buy price, you have the opportunity to add a further amount if you have the cash available. This amount ideally needs to be equal to the payments you have previously put in. For example, if you had bought using three amounts valued at £50,000, and the market presented the opportunity to add, you would add another £50,000.

There could be as many as 10 further opportunities to add, depending on the depth and duration of the bear market. One thing to remember with this strategy is that even though income is accessible, my recommendation would be to not touch the money for at least 10 years. After a decade had passed, you could then start an income withdrawal program.

Final thoughts on the S&P 500 Strategy

The S&P 500 Strategy is extremely time friendly, perfect for leaving a legacy and an excellent way to achieve a decent return on capital outside your ISA and SIPP. It's a strategy that could net you an annual return of 7–10% over the long term. It's very simple and straightforward and the rules I've suggested are not set in stone. The key thing here is that you understand the principle, which is to end up making a return almost equal to the return of the S&P 500, using capital outside your ISA and SIPP investments.

This is an investment that should be grown over 50 to 100 years, or even longer. If you are going to take an income from it, try not to touch the account for at least 5 years and when you eventually do start to take an income from it, aim to keep your withdrawals to a minimum, maybe 1–3% per year.

Okay, so are you ready for the final chapter? Yes, regrettably it's the last chapter, however I promise that it contains information that I'm sure you'll find extremely valuable. I'm going to be sharing with you a golden opportunity, ideal for investors 'in the know' and I'll also share with you how you could potentially profit from it.

You're also going to see stacked up evidence suggesting that now is probably a very good time to invest and together we are going to examine the topic of lost decades, why the long term is so important, the resilience of the markets and how the market has historically had periods of strength after periods of weakness. I'd be very surprised if this final chapter doesn't get you excited. Let's go and look at what could be…

12: A Golden Opportunity

*'We simply attempt to be fearful when others are greedy and to
be greedy only when others are fearful.'*
– Warren Buffett

In this final chapter I'm going to share with you details of an
investment opportunity that could seriously boost your portfolio over
the coming years. This same opportunity is right under everyone's
noses but because they have not been informed about it, they have
no idea it exists. There is an English Proverb that sums this up
beautifully: 'Some men go through a forest and see no firewood.'

How to spot investment opportunities

Most people would agree that recently has been a difficult time to
invest. However, it's worth remembering that there are investment
opportunities in the difficult periods, as well as the good times. For
all the worry felt by some that the world is facing financial problems
from which it will never recover, history tells us differently.

True, there are new issues, including the shifting power from West
to East, and the huge impact of the internet on globalisation. But the
challenges faced by markets today are no different than those of the
Great Depression in the 1930s or the crisis years of the 1970s.

Just as in those decades, the crises facing developed world markets today include government indebtedness, high unemployment and economic stagnation. But both the 1930s and 1970s were followed by successive decades of massive growth, a return to strong levels of employment – and for investors, excellent investment returns.

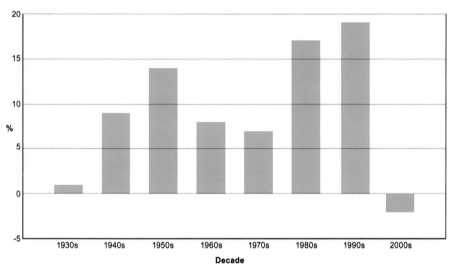

Source: Thomson One, Jan 7, 2010.
Past performance is not a guarantee of future results.

If history has any lesson to teach us about lost investment decades, it is that there is a recurring nature to global stock markets. Abandoning the markets may have been an understandable response in the early 1940s or 1980s, but what a mistake it would have been!

The best time to invest

Stock markets have suffered two sharp falls in the past 10 years, and in many cases remain below their previous peak – some have even called this a lost decade. The last time the markets went through such an extended period of underperformance was in the 1960s and 1970s.

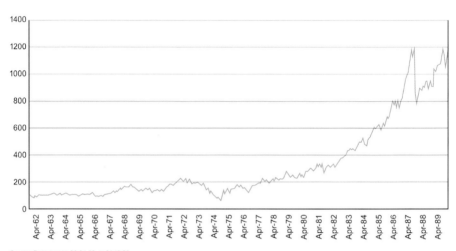

Source: Datastream, 30.04.62. to 31.12.89.
This graph is based on the FTSE All-Share Price Index and uses the earliest available figures from the 1960's.
Please remember that past performance is not an indication of what will happen in the future.

By the start of the 1980s, many investors were shell-shocked by their experience and convinced that things could only get worse. However, someone who looked beyond the difficult conditions and bought when prices were low would have then enjoyed one of the best periods of extended outperformance in the market's history. This performance adds to the theory that the best time to invest can be when it feels the most difficult to do so.

Why is thinking long term so important?

One of the important things to remember is that you shouldn't be worried by short-term fluctuations. It's easier said than done of course, but the point is that when you are investing for the long term, you should have plenty of time to ride out the market uncertainty.

In the case of the UK stock market, as represented by the FTSE All-Share Index, this has had an average annual return of 7.2% over the last 49 years (to 30/11/11). Don't forget, this period includes Black Monday, Black Wednesday, the dotcom bubble, the Russian financial crisis, the Asian financial crisis and the oil crisis – so there were definitely some downs as well as ups.

The market repeatedly overcomes adversity

The US's Standard & Poor's 500 Composite Index has experienced its share of shock events, but for many decades the market has demonstrated an ability to overcome adversity. The market's resilience has been particularly evident in its climb from the March 2009 low.

Rarely does a year go by without a crisis of some sort and in 2011, the market had to deal with several shocking and surprising events, including the unrest in the Middle East and North Africa, and the earthquake and tsunami in Japan, which resulted in staggering loss of life and a crisis at a nuclear power plant.

A look at about 50 years of the S&P 500's history (see chart on page 228) shows that there's been no shortage of traumatic events. But, decade after decade, the market has demonstrated its ability to climb a wall of worry. Even since the market's low in March 2009, the S&P has demonstrated its strength in the face of issues ranging from the flash crash to high unemployment.

Many of the events depicted on the chart have been traumatic and costly. The market, however, has not only survived, but thrived. For

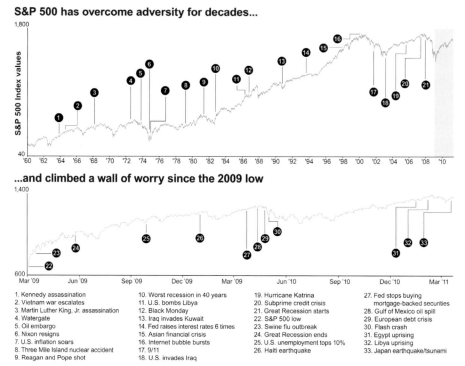

S&P 500 has overcome adversity for decades...

...and climbed a wall of worry since the 2009 low

1. Kennedy assassination
2. Vietnam war escalates
3. Martin Luther King, Jr. assassination
4. Watergate
5. Oil embargo
6. Nixon resigns
7. U.S. inflation soars
8. Three Mile Island nuclear accident
9. Reagan and Pope shot
10. Worst recession in 40 years
11. U.S. bombs Libya
12. Black Monday
13. Iraq invades Kuwait
14. Fed raises interest rates 6 times
15. Asian financial crisis
16. Internet bubble bursts
17. 9/11
18. U.S. invades Iraq
19. Hurricane Katrina
20. Subprime credit crisis
21. Great Recession starts
22. S&P 500 low
23. Swine flu outbreak
24. Great Recession ends
25. U.S. unemployment tops 10%
26. Haiti earthquake
27. Fed stops buying mortgage-backed securities
28. Gulf of Mexico oil spill
29. European debt crisis
30. Flash crash
31. Egypt uprising
32. Libya uprising
33. Japan earthquake/tsunami

The specific periods depicted are as follows: 1/1/60-3/31/11 (top chart) and 3/9/09-3/31/11 (bottom chart). The S&P 500 Index is unmanaged.

more than a century, the US market has endured wars, recessions, assassinations, scandals and natural disasters and each time it has come back. Through it all, the market has demonstrated remarkable strength and resilience in the face of challenges.

Did you know that there are periods of strength after weakness?

Another piece of research that proves useful is the Barclays Gilt Study of 2009. History, once again, shows that the returns enjoyed by investors who can overcome their instinct to seek a safe haven in difficult times could be significantly higher in the long term. When you look at history, you find that extended periods of poor performance have almost always led to periods of above-average performance. As investment in equities should be viewed as a medium to long-term savings vehicle, the study looked at returns over 10 year periods, as illustrated in this table.

Average annual returns over 10 years	%	Average annual return in the 10 years immediately afterwards	%
1906 - 1915	-0.2	1916 - 1925	+3.9
1907 - 1916	-3.7	1917 - 1926	+6.5
1908 - 1917	-3.8	1918 - 1927	+9.1
1909 - 1918	-3.5	1919 - 1928	+10.3
1910 - 1919	-3.8	1920 - 1929	+7.8
1911 - 1920	-7.9	1921 -1930	+12.8
1912 - 1921	-5.1	1922 - 1931	+7.6
1913 - 1922	-1.9	1923 - 1932	+7.5
1914 - 1923	-1.3	1924 - 1933	+9.6
1965 - 1974	-6.0	1975 - 1984	+17.4
1967 - 1976	-0.3	1977 - 1986	+14.6
1968 - 1977	-0.2	1978 - 1987	+12.0
1969 - 1978	-3.5	1979 - 1988	+12.4
1970 - 1979	-2.3	1980 - 1989	+15.6
1972 - 1981	-2.4	1982 - 1991	+13.2
1973 - 1982	-1.2	1983 - 1992	+12.7
1999 - 2008	-1.5		
Average	**-2.9%**	**Average**	**+10.8%**

Source: Barclays Capital Gilt Study 2009 (based on FTSE All Share index and includes dividends reinvested).

The Barclays study shows that since 1899 there have been 17 lost decades (10 year periods of negative performance) with an average annual return of -2.9%. This includes the most recent decade (to the end of 2008), where UK equities suffered average annual returns of -1.5%.

Notice that each of the decades immediately following a lost decade has provided positive average annual total returns, with an average of 10.8% per annum. This data suggests that over the next decade we are likely to see above average returns.

The ability to recover and advance after extended periods of decline

A look back at the modern history of the S&P 500 reveals a pattern similar to UK equities. Over time, the market has demonstrated strength in the face of adversity and long-term investors have been rewarded.

S&P 500, rolling 10-year periods, December 31st 1927 – December 31st 2010

Best 10-year periods		Next 10 years	Worst 10-year periods		Next 10 years
10 years ended...	Average annual total return	Average annual total return	10 years ended...	Average annual total return	Average annual total return
1951	17.26%	16.42%	1937	0.00%	9.61
1952	17.06	13.44	1938	-0.93	7.25
1954	17.09	12.82	1939	-0.08	9.15
1955	16.67	11.07	1940	1.78	13.36
1956	18.40	9.20	1941	6.44	17.26
1957	16.41	12.85	1946	4.41	18.40
1958	20.04	10.01	1973	6.00	10.66
1959	19.34	7.82	1974	1.23	14.81
1960	16.15	8.18	1975	3.27	14.34
1961	16.42	7.06	1976	6.64	13.84
1963	15.91	6.00	1977	3.60	15.28
1988	16.32	19.19	1978	3.17	16.32
1989	17.54	18.19	1979	5.88	17.54
1991	17.58	12.93	1981	6.49	17.58
1992	16.15	9.34	1982	6.72	16.15
1997	18.02	5.91	2007	5.91	N/A
1998	19.19	-1.38	2008	-1.38	N/A
1999	18.19	-0.95	2009	-0.95	N/A
2000	17.44	1.42	2010	1.42	N/A
Average	17.43	9.45	Average	3.14	14.10

9.45% Average return after best 10-year periods

10.74% Average return for all 10-year periods

14.10% Average return after worst 10-year periods

Based on average annual total returns of 74 rolling 10-year periods, divided into quartiles. The range of returns for each quartile is as follows: Quartile 1 (top/best quartile), 15.91% to 20.04%; Quartile 2, 11.06% to 15.28%; Quartile 3, 7.06% to 10.66%; and Quartile 4, –1.38% to 6.72%. The average return for the years after the best and worst periods is the average of the average annual total return of the periods following each period in the top and bottom quartile, respectively. Data are not available for future 10-year periods; therefore, the last return for the "next 10 years" is for the period 12/31/00–12/31/10. The S&P 500 Index is unmanaged, and its results include reinvested dividends and/or distributions but do not reflect the effect of sales charges, commissions, account fees, expenses or taxes.

The chart depicts returns for 10 year periods that fall into the top quartile and bottom quartile since December 31st 1927. A look at the 10 year periods can be instructive, given that the market recently recorded its worst decade, registering an average annual decline of 1.4% for the 10 years ending December 31st 2008.

The data for the worst 10 year periods show that the market has demonstrated the ability to recover and advance after extended periods of decline. For example, after a decade that fell into the bottom quartile, the following decade provided returns that were not only higher and positive, but often higher than the 10.7% average return for all rolling 10 year periods since 1927.

Final thoughts

In this final chapter, we've discovered that, for all the worry felt by some that the world is facing unprecedented challenges from which it will never recover, history tells us differently. For example, both the 1930s and 1970s were followed by successive decades of massive growth, a return to strong levels of employment and, for investors, excellent investment returns. We also learned in this chapter what a mistake the investors who abandoned the market in the early 1940s or 1980s made.

In the past, looking beyond the difficult conditions and buying when prices are low would have resulted in enjoying some of the best periods of extended outperformance in the market's history. Remember that the best time to invest can often be when it feels the most difficult to do so. If history does repeat itself, the next ten years is probably going to be a decade of outperformance – which means that now could be a perfect time to be investing, as long as you are doing so for the long haul.

If like me, you have a long-term investment outlook, you could say that now is a golden opportunity for investors 'in the know'. There has never been a better time to invest. This really is a great time for DIY investors who are looking to make a reasonable rate of return over the coming years.

It is now time for me to sign off. I bid you farewell and look forward to possibly meeting you in the near future. I am already excited about hearing your amazing story of how you conquered adversity, broke through and ended up realising your financial dreams. Thank you for reading this book and I hope that you have enjoyed reading it as much as I enjoyed writing it. My friend, I wish you health, wealth and happiness.

THANK YOU

Thank you for buying and reading this book and trusting me to offer something of value. I sincerely hope you use these concepts to achieve your financial objectives and I'd be thrilled to hear about your experiences. Either go to our website www.ISACO.co.uk and click on the contact us link or send me an email: Stephen@ISACO.co.uk.

I hope you consider subscribing to our 'Grow Your Wealth' blog at http://web.isaco.co.uk/blog. It would be a huge honour if you decide to subscribe as it would prove that this book has had a positive impact on you. Naturally, I'd like you to eventually become one of our premium clients, but even if you choose not to, I sincerely wish you all the very best with your future investments.

Warm regards,

Stephen

Appendix 1: About ISACO

ISACO specialises in ISA and SIPP Investment and is the pioneer of 'Shadow Investment'; an easy way to grow your ISA and SIPP at low cost. Together with our clients, we have an estimated £57 million actively invested in ISAs and pensions[44]. Clients like us because we have a great track record of 'beating' the FTSE 100[45]. Over the last 16 years, we've outperformed the Footsie by 60.2% and over the last 5 years, we've averaged 14.5% each year versus the FTSE 100's 8.8%. You can find us at www.ISACO.co.uk.

What is Shadow Investment?

Picking the right fund for your ISA and SIPP is not exactly the easiest job in the world. And knowing 'when' to buy and 'when' to exit is even more difficult! Our 'Shadow Investment' Service is here to help. Our service allows you to look over our shoulder and buy the same funds that we are buying.

When we are thinking of buying a fund, we alert you so that you have the opportunity to buy it on the same day that we buy it. We also tell you about when we are planning to exit the fund. You control your investment account, not us. You can start small and invest as little or as much money as you like.

By knowing what we are buying, when we are buying and when we are exiting, throughout the year you can mirror our movements and in effect replicate our trades. This means you have the opportunity to benefit from exactly the same investment returns that we get. Our investment aims are 10–12% per year.

We are totally independent, fully transparent and FCA compliant. We're warm, friendly and highly responsive and it's a very personal service that gives you direct access to the Sutherland brothers; ISACO's two founders.

Who are ISACO's clients?

Clients who benefit most from our service have over £250,000 actively invested and the majority of them are wealthy retirees, business owners, self-employed professionals and corporate executives. We also have clients from the financial services sector, such as IFAs and wealth managers.

Do you have questions?

To have all your questions answered, call 0800 170 7750 or email us at: info@ISACO.co.uk.

Appendix 2: About the Author

Stephen Sutherland is ISACO's lead investor and Chief Investment Strategist. He is also the author of *Liquid Millionaire* and *How to Make Money in ISAs and SIPPs*. Stephen is a commentator on business television and radio, and in personal finance newspapers, magazines and other market commentator mediums.

Stephen aims is to buy 'best of breed' funds that exhibit superior sustainable growth potential and hold them for as long as they demonstrate outperformance. His investment style is to seek out only those funds that have the greatest potential for swift price rises from the moment they are purchased. He can be reached directly at Stephen@ISACO.co.uk.

Appendix 3: The Value of Advice, Tips and Ideas

Whether it's a tip, suggestion, recommendation to buy, an investment idea or personalised financial advice, they all carry a value. The question is; what is the information worth? Everybody knows that some advice is going to be worthless, whereas other information could prove priceless. So, what is the best way to determine the value of the information you are being given? My suggestion would be to use the four points listed below as your guide:

1) The source has an impressive investment track record
2) Their own money is invested in their recommendations
3) You are alerted when to buy and when to exit
4) You receive daily market updates

The range of people who can give you a tip or recommendation is vast. They can be friends, family and work associates or full time investment professionals. Advice can come from an individual or company but to keep things simple, when we examine the four things to look for we will refer to the individual or company as the 'source'.

My suggestion would be to check any sources that you're thinking of using against these four key points.

Also be aware that apart from qualified, authorised and registered firms, brokers, banks and investment advisers, most of these sources will not be policed by the Financial Conduct Authority (FCA). This means that if you choose to take a recommendation from a non-authorised and unregulated source, you are likely to receive less governance, less transparency and less protection should something go wrong.

Investment ideas from the web

When you search on the internet for help with investment selection, you'll see many financial services company websites offering things such as:

Premier Selection from Bestinvest:
> https://select.bestinvest.co.uk/investment-guidance/free-guides/premier-selection

The Select List from Fidelity:
> https://www.fidelity.co.uk/investor/funds/find-funds/select-list/default.page

and Investment Ideas from Hargreaves Lansdown:
> http://www.hl.co.uk/funds/fund-news-and-investment-ideas/latest-investment-ideas

You'll also find plenty of tips and advice on sites like Yahoo! Finance:
> http://uk.finance.yahoo.com/news/category-newspaper-tips-round-up/

Motley Fool:
> www.fool.co.uk

MoneyWeek:
> http://www.moneyweek.com/investment-advice/share-tips

and Citywire:
> www.citywire.co.uk

Tips and Ideas from Newspapers and magazines

The popular personal finance website, This is Money (www.thisismoney.co.uk), part of the Daily Mail, Mail on Sunday & Metro Media Group, offers share and fund tips for free.

Investors Chronicle (www.investorschronicle.co.uk) is a personal finance magazine and website that provides share tips and fund tips and offers access to a range of investors' portfolios, including Mr Bearbull, Simon Thompson, Chris Dillow, David Stevenson and John Baron. As I've already said, being able to follow real life investors' portfolios carries a lot of weight, especially if they have a great track record, so these are all worth looking at in greater depth. Through *Investors Chronicle,* you can also access broker tips and tips from the press.

The *Daily Telegraph* (www.telegraph.co.uk/finance/personalfinance/ investing/shares-and-stock-tips) also offers stocks and shares tips. You'll also get plenty of tips and ideas from newspapers such as *The Sunday Times* (www.thesundaytimes.co.uk), *Daily Mail* (www.dailymail.co.uk), *The Guardian* (www.guardian.co.uk) and *The Financial Times* (www.ft.com). *Shares* (www.sharesmagazine. co.uk) is a stock trading magazine offering lots of share tips, and personal finance magazine *Money Observer* (www.moneyobserver .com) also offers stock tips. *Moneywise* magazine (www.moneywise. co.uk) also offers suggestions that may prove useful.

Newsletter tipping services

If you type 'investment newsletter tipping services' into Google, you'll see companies such as MoneyWeek (www.moneyweek.com/ shop/premium-services), who offer newsletters written by real life investors, Quantum Leap (www.quantumleapnewsletter.co.uk) and Trident Confidential (www.tridentconfidential.com).

Two other companies that may fall into this bracket are Fat Prophets (www.fatprophets.co.uk) and Faraday Research (www.faraday research.co.uk).Newsletters are normally subscription-based services; if they're free, they usually offer little value.

Financial adviser/investment adviser

IFAs, wealth managers and investment advisers are regulated and policed by the FCA, which means that they have to adhere to strict rules and guidelines. Regulation by the FCA means the highest level of governance and transparency. It also tells you that if you do business with these kinds of sources, you have a certain amount of protection should something go wrong. The challenge that advisers in the financial services industry face is that they come under heavy criticism and are generally mistrusted.

Sadly, bad practice still exists in the investment advice industry. This can range from professional incompetence – including ignorance of the body of science of markets – to sharp or shady practice. Unfortunately, poor investment performance is a major challenge within the industry. Many advisers aim for a paltry 5% annual growth on behalf of their clients as this is roughly the real return of the UK stock market over the last century[46].

However, most advisers underperform the market[47], with potentially serious consequences for their clients. Why do so many underperform? Aren't these people supposed to be investment experts? My take is that they fail to beat the benchmarks because most of them are not full time professional investors who study and understand the markets. As most advisers underperform, it means that the majority will achieve less than a 5% annual return.

Even though many advisers should be avoided, not all of them are bad. Some advisers are exceptionally talented and have their clients' best interests in mind at all times. These advisers are rare individuals and are worth their weight in gold. We have three such IFAs as clients. Morwenna Clarke (married to Lee Clarke, author of *The Trusted Adviser* – a great book!), Neil Sutherland and Iain Cahill – who are all incredibly competent, highly likeable and extremely trustworthy.

New regulations introduced on January 1ˢᵗ 2013 called the Retail Distribution Review (RDR) should have helped remove some of the investment problems that have been negatively affecting the industry. This is good news for private investors. In particular, the RDR has made paying for financial advice fairer and clearer. For example, these new regulations ban advisers from receiving commission for new investment advice and should ensure best advice for consumers, rather than advisers pointing them in the direction of a service or product that pays the highest commission.

What is the Retail Distribution Review?

The RDR is a key part of the Financial Conduct Authority's (FCA) consumer protection strategy. The idea behind it is that you'll have more confidence and trust if you do decide to seek retirement and investment planning advice from a qualified adviser. Since January 1st 2013, you'll have been more likely to be offered a transparent and fair charging system for the advice given. You should also be crystal clear about the service you receive and the advice is more likely to come from highly respected professionals.

To achieve this, the FCA has published new rules under the RDR that require:

- Advisory firms to disclose and separately charge clients for their services.
- Advisory firms to clearly describe their services as either 'independent' or 'restricted'.
- Individual advisers to adhere to consistent professional standards, including a code of ethics.

These changes apply to all advisers regardless of the type of firm they work for (banks, product providers, independent financial advisers, wealth managers or stockbrokers). The new professionalism requirements under the RDR aim to improve levels of confidence and build trust in the investment industry. For more information go to http://www.fca.org.uk/your-fca/documents/fsa-rdr-ind-advice-factsheet.

Appendix 4: Junior ISAs

Junior ISAs (JISAs) are fantastic! They can give your child or grandchild a head start in life and provide an excellent tax-efficient way of saving for a child's future. You can invest in a JISA each year and the money invested will grow over time and be available to the child on their 18th birthday.

If you opted for a stocks and shares JISA, it could be worth nearly £108,000* if you invested £300 a month from the birth of a child until they reach the age of 18. The other benefit is that there will be no income or capital gains tax (CGT) to pay.

*This projection is for illustrative purposes and assumes a growth rate of 6%, after charges and is not guaranteed.

Here is a quick summary of some JISA basics:
- A JISA is set up in the child's name by a parent or guardian
- You can set up a stocks and shares JISA or cash JISA or a combination of both
- Any investment growth is free of income or capital gains tax (CGT)
- For 2014/2015 the investment limit is £3,840
- Anyone can contribute to a child's account at anytime through the year
- Money is locked away until the child reaches the age of 18
- The child is the beneficial owner of the JISA

If you set up a JISA on a fund supermarket platform, you'll be able to invest in the same range of funds that you can invest in for adult ISAs. That means you could, in effect, buy the same funds for your child or grandchild as you are investing in for yourself. JISAs are available to all children who missed out on the Child Trust Fund (CTF). Parents, grandparents, family and friends can contribute up to £3,840 a year for the tax year 2014/ 2015.

Money is locked away for the child, who can withdraw the proceeds when they reach adulthood, and they are extremely tax-efficient, just like an adult ISA. Unlike regular ISAs, a child can only have one cash JISA and one stocks and shares JISA at any time. You don't have to take out a new JISA each tax year. The child's JISAs do not have to be held by the same provider – and accounts can be transferred between providers providing all the relevant JISA conditions are met.

The biggest difference between JISAs and CTFs is the lack of a CTF voucher. The CTF voucher was a guarantee from the Government to invest at least £250 on the opening of a CTF and a further £250 on a child's seventh birthday, as an incentive to start saving. JISAs unfortunately offer no such incentive.

The good news however, is that the maximum amount you can invest each year, £3,840 (2014/2015), is triple the amount you could invest in a CTF. To help you learn everything you need to know about JISAs, I've put together a list of frequently asked questions.

Q: My child already has a CTF, what should I do?
A: In December 2013, the Treasury announced that from April 2015 parents will be able to transfer cash from a CTF to a Junior ISA.

Since November 1st 2011, the annual CTF allowance matches the annual JISA allowance. For 2014/2015 the allowance is £3,840.

Q: Who is eligible for a JISA?

A: Any child resident in the UK who wasn't eligible for a CTF:

- Children born on or after January 3rd 2011
- Children (aged under 18) born on or before August 31st 2002
- Children born on or between September 1st 2002 and January 2nd 2011 who didn't qualify for a CTF. Note that most children born between these dates did qualify for a CTF

Q: Who can contribute?

A: Once a parent or guardian opens a JISA for their child, anyone – friend or family – is able to make a contribution up to the annual limit. Decisions on where and when to invest ISA contributions are made by the parent or guardian who is the registered contact for the account, but the account is held in the child's name. The money is ring-fenced for the child until they are 18 – no withdrawals are permitted before then, except in the event of terminal illness or death.

Q: What is the definition of parental responsibility?

A: Parental responsibility means the child's natural parent, or someone who has legally adopted the child who has been granted parental responsibility by the court or a local authority.

Q: What are the tax rules in a JISA?

A: A JISA, like an adult ISA, is not an investment itself but simply a tax wrapper that protects the investment from personal liability for tax. Any returns made with a JISA are not subject to capital gains tax (CGT) or income tax for both the child and their parents or guardians. The income tax rule for gifts from parents to their children does not apply when investing into a JISA.

Therefore, if your children are lucky enough to receive substantial gifts, it would be more tax-efficient for those financial gifts to use the JISA allowance, primarily. Using the JISA allowance does not affect the child's eligibility to open an adult cash ISA when they reach 16 years old.

Q: What are the tax benefits on JISAs?
A: Cash JISAs will receive interest without deduction of tax. A stocks and shares JISA will grow free of any potential CGT tax liability. Interest income, such as that from the Government or corporate bond holdings, will be free of income tax. However, dividends from shares are paid with 10% tax deducted and this cannot be reclaimed, even inside a JISA. Note: tax rules can change over time and the benefits to your child will depend on their individual circumstances.

Q: What other benefits come from investing in a JISA?
A: JISAs can give your child or grandchild a head start in life and provide an excellent tax-efficient way of saving for them. JISAs were launched in November 2011, which means that they are a fairly new, tax-free way of saving for your child's future. Here are the 4 main benefits of JISAs:

1) **Huge choice** – If you choose to buy your JISA from a fund supermarket, you have a huge choice of funds from many different providers.
2) **Flexibility** – you can select more than one fund for your JISA and include funds from more than one fund provider.

3) **Quick set up** – just one application form per child to complete.

4) **Simplified management** – view all your account details, place deals and view balances online, 24 hours a day.

Q: Can a JISA be transferred?

A: It is possible to transfer JISAs between providers and also transfer monies from one JISA type to another e.g. from a cash JISA to a stocks and shares JISA.

Q: Can I access the money held in a JISA?

A: No, you cannot access the money held in a JISA. Like a CTF, the account is set up for the child and only they can access the money when they reach 18 years.

Q: Do I have to take out a new JISA, with a new provider, each tax year?

A: No. Unlike an adult ISA where you can take out a new ISA each tax year, all the money in your stocks and shares or cash JISA is kept with one provider (although you can transfer the funds to another provider at any time if you wish).

Q: How does topping up your JISA investment work?

A: You can add to your JISA at any time and can normally top up online by simply logging into your JISA account. You can also call your provider and pay by debit card or cheque. I suggest you always double check because topping up may differ from provider to provider. Some, e.g. Friendly Societies, may be more restrictive.

Q: What about friends and family top ups?

Friends and family members can make payments to the account but the investment decisions must be made by the parent or guardian. For lump sum payments, you have to complete a JISA top up form. A cheque can be made by any friend or family member. Alternatively, lump sum payments can normally be made by debit card over the phone.

You can often set up a monthly savings plan by simply completing a JISA application form. You can usually set up more than one monthly savings plan so grandparents, friends and other family members can all contribute to the JISA.

Q: What happens when the child reaches 16?

A: The child can start making limited investment decisions such as switching between funds in their JISA, but the instructions must be given by the parent or guardian. It will be possible for the child to remove the adult name and take over management of the JISA account. If you are setting up a JISA for a child between the ages of 16 and 18 the account must be set up by a parent or guardian. When a child turns 16 they can also open a cash ISA in addition to their Junior ISA.

Q: What happens when the child reaches 18?

A: As soon as the child reaches their 18th birthday, JISAs automatically become adult ISAs. The parent or guardian's name is then removed from the account but the named child remains the beneficial owner. The provider writes to the named child on their 18th birthday, confirming that they now own an adult ISA. All investment decisions must then be made by the named child.

Payments can no longer be made by family or friends and all monthly savings plans will stop, however, they can be restarted by the named child. The JISA will no longer be visible in the parent or guardian's online account and the maximum investment limit will rise to the adult annual ISA allowance.

Q: How can I buy a JISA?

A: If your child is under 16, someone with parental responsibility (for example, a parent or step-parent) must open the JISA for them. Children aged 16 to 18 can open their own JISA. But someone with parental responsibility could still open the account for them. A range of fund supermarkets, banks, building societies, credit unions, friendly societies and stockbrokers offer JISAs.

To open a JISA you need to:

- Choose the type of JISA; cash or stocks and shares account (or both)
- Check which account providers offer the type of account you want
- Choose the provider – bank, building society, broker or fund supermarket
- Get an application form from the provider.

To discover more about JISAs, go to http://web.isaco.co.uk/blog/?Tag=Junior+ISAs and http://www.hmrc.gov.uk/.

Appendix 5: Book reviews

"With his newest book, Stephen Sutherland is ready to spread the wealth! Having realized the power of the stock market in his own portfolio as well as his clients', Sutherland takes the time to reveal some of his 'secrets' for choosing the market's best funds.

I found this book incredibly easy to read and understand. Sutherland spends time on the concepts that matter. For anyone looking to take a more active role in their investing, *How to Make Money in ISAs and SIPPs* is a great resource . . . and an easy read. It walks you through the benefits of the UK's two tax-efficient accounts before revealing some actionable strategies you can use to unlock the power of the market.

Your brain is often the enemy of your returns, and I'm glad Sutherland spent time identifying some of the behavioral shortcomings investors face. Make no mistake: Buy-and-hold investing is not dead! Even though Sutherland's approach is more technical than what we preach at The Motley Fool, he values consistency, performance, and tenure in management teams . . . and we Fools can't argue with that!

Jill Ralph, Managing Director, The Motley Fool UK

"Stephen, thanks for producing such an excellent book. You should be rightly proud of it. It was a pleasure to read it (three times). *How to Make Money in ISAs and SIPPs* is a MUST READ for anyone who invests money in funds. The book takes you from the basics of understanding the ISA and SIPP wrapper, through to the all important aspect of how to pick good funds and manage your portfolio. It is written in an easy to follow, logical order which covers the subject in a very comprehensive way, catering for anyone less familiar with the subject, right through to the more seasoned investor.

The process of picking good funds is covered in detail in Chapter 6 and the information in this chapter alone is worth the price of the book. There are many graphical examples included in the book, which aids the understanding of the concepts discussed, including step by step screen shots detailing how to check a fund's performance and characteristics. I was delighted to see that Stephen also covered the psychology of investing within Chapter 9. In my opinion, as a more seasoned investor, this is one of the critical aspects that an investor must understand if they are going to be successful in the markets.

Stephen's enthusiasm for the markets and the depth of his knowledge on the subject are clear throughout the book. His positive attitude to life shines through right from the outset and this combination of knowledge and enthusiasm has produced a book which is easy to read and understand, whether you are a seasoned participant in the market or completely new to the subject. I'd go as far as to say turning to the next page is compelling. That's not something that can be said for many books on finance. I also think this book should be compulsory reading for all senior secondary school children as they set out into the world. I certainly wish it had been around when I was at that stage.

The book should at the very least, be on everybody's investment book shelf but it would serve you better being on your desk. It's an excellent book which I will be referring to over and over again. 5 stars."

Ray Hughes, ISACO Client, Entrepreneur and Private Investor

"A thorough and very useful guide to investing in ISAs and SIPPs, and well timed. There are now a huge number of 'orphan investors' without an IFA as a direct result of RDR, and the information provided in this book gives them much needed support. Easy to read and follow, and put into context throughout. The information on charges is particularly useful."

Josh Ausden, Editor, FE Trustnet

"Dear Stephen, firstly I would like to complain as I could not stop reading your new book! My plan was to have a quick look at it then read it on a long flight later this week! I will need to buy another book now! Seriously though, I think your book is excellent. I found it's written in a simple way to understand so that non-financial professional people like me can grasp the points.

I have lots of books about investing and mostly they are complicated and to be honest, boring. I enjoyed reading your new book and could not put it down – it just makes so much sense. I guess the part of the book I most enjoyed was 'Chapter 9: Beyond Greed and Fear' – I found myself saying 'that's me' and I can fully recognise this behavioural finance, which is a very interesting subject. I would rate the book with 5 stars.

It's now been four years since I became a client of yours, I fully believe in your concept and have made good returns, it's a great system. I also love the fact that you have very kindly donated your royalties from the new book to the Christie Charity. Very well done to you and your team and keep up the good work."

David Mountain, ISACO Client and Engineer

"At last a common-sense, easy to understand book that proves you don't need to have an MBA or be a financial whizz kid to build a healthy retirement pot. And you can do it all using legitimate tax breaks in the form of SIPPs and ISAs that the government and HMRC fully approve of. Stephen estimates he has spent over 20,000 hours perfecting his investment technique, but his book allows you to learn many of his simple skills in the space of a few hours.

This book is a worthwhile read for the new or fairly experienced private investor – and maybe even a few so-called professional investors. You don't have to want or believe you can be a millionaire from reading it, but it will help you take control of your own savings and make better investment decisions. This book could be the best investment you've ever made."

Lawrence Gosling, Founding Editor of Investment Week

"One day I realised that to secure my future, I would have to learn more about investing some of my hard-earned money. I read several books and courses but found it difficult to glean much. I didn't learn much from a few financial investment advisors I met and considerably less from some bank advisors.

As for most of the graphs they produced whilst advising me, I was more confused than ever.

Then along came Stephen Sutherland and his company ISACO with his book *Liquid Millionaire* and then his new book 'How to Make Money in ISAs and SIPPs' with the sub-title, 'Tax-Efficient Investment Made Easy'.

Stephen's books were a breath of fresh air to me – full of knowledge, detail and his expertise, in fact a work of art in explaining how to improve your returns on every pound you invest and also how you can avoid some of the high and hidden charges that can reduce your returns.

A huge bonus is how Stephen writes in such an easily understood and interesting style.

The documented proof of his record in helping others to improve their investments made me realise I had found the mentor I needed to help secure my financial goals. Stephen's book allows you to be a 'fly on the wall – look over his shoulder' at exactly how he selects his investments.

My advice to you is to read the book (I give it a 5 star rating) – then take action on Stephen's advice. You might also decide to become a personal client as I did, which allows me to simply follow the decisions he makes, it's so easy. Another really great thing I like, is that he keeps all his clients informed of everything he is doing investment-wise every single day, which takes just 3 to 4 minutes to read. If you do read the book it could change your life and your financial success – as it has mine and continues to do so."

Bob Sweeney, ISACO Client and Private Investor

"What a wonderful book. The arguments regarding investing via ISAs and SIPPs are well argued and fascinating."

Alan Miller, SCM Private Chief Investment Officer

"I became a client of Stephen's after reading his first book *Liquid Millionaire* in 2010. I read a lot of the financial press and get confused by most of it. Stephen's very clear and straightforward approach seemed to me to have real integrity. I have not regretted my decision. I just wish I had found Stephen, and his brother Paul, ten years earlier!!

Practice makes perfect, and *How to Make Money in ISAs and SIPPs* is an even better and clearer read than Stephen's first book. His style is engagingly free of jargon, and is very easy to read. The book is very well structured. He explains what ISAs and SIPPs are and why they are so important. Importantly, he goes into the all too often grey area of fees and how to minimise them. But most importantly, he clearly explains the critical importance of when to invest in which funds AND when to exit from them.

There is no doubt this book will greatly help a novice investor, and even experienced ones, to pick funds and time them accurately. Personally I leave all of that to Stephen and Paul, and so far their track record is very impressive indeed. But whether you let them take the strain or do it yourself, read this book – it can only help. I would unequivocally give it a 5 star rating!!"

John W. Cornwell, ISACO Client and Consultant Chartered Town Planner

"A very readable book dispelling a lot of myths that stand between investors and financial security. This book is particularly suitable for beginners, the people who know little about investing but who stand to gain most. It is set out logically so that you progress seamlessly from one topic to the next, learning all the way."

Rodney Hobson, Bestselling Author, *Shares Made Simple, The Dividend Investor, How to Build a Share Portfolio, Understanding Company News* and *Small Companies, Big Profits*

"I wish that I had read this book 20 years ago. It would have radically changed my saving and investing strategies and would have dramatically improved my financial position today. Stephen Sutherland's book *How to Make Money in ISAs and SIPPs* has opened my eyes to the major benefits of investing in ISAs and SIPPs, and in his sections on myths, dispelled a number of erroneous ideas I had.

I particularly liked his informal writing style; it is almost like having a friend by your side giving you their advice. The book is packed with useful information and guides the reader on how to choose suitable funds to invest and how to minimise their charges and costs. My favourite chapters were *Beyond Greed and Fear* because most of the content was new to me; *How to Manage Your Portfolio* because it identifies resources that I never knew existed and *Creating an Income for Life* because it has provoked me into thinking about my timescales for investment.

I also liked the fact that Stephen describes his results in both his good and bad years and how his investment approach has significantly developed and improved over the period that he has studied ISAs and SIPPs. This book is a must buy for anyone who is serious about building up wealth for their retirement, or for helping their children invest for their future. 5 stars!"

Jeff Hall, ISACO Client and Business Owner

"I'm not sure what's controversial about this. Make as much money as you can in the market, and pay as little of it as possible to the tax man. If you blow the last part, you might as well have blown the first part. So, wrap your high-performing portfolio in tax protection with the ideas in this book."

Jason Kelly, Bestselling Author of *The Neatest Little Guide to Stock Market Investing*

"I found this book extremely informative for investors, particularly those investing in ISAs and SIPPs, and for others who are trying to optimize their investment returns. It explains simply and in sufficient detail for the less knowledgeable how to take advantage of these tax-efficient schemes, how to ensure you're invested in the best funds and manage your portfolio effectively and how to determine whether we're heading for a bull or bear market i.e. when to get in, stay in or get out. It also suggests how to create regular income from your investments but is not for those wanting to earn a quick buck; it takes a long term view.

Before becoming an ISACO client I read Stephen's previous book *Liquid Millionaire,* which led me to believe that 'shadow investing' for our ISAs was the way to go. I feel much better informed now, particularly on selecting the best funds, how to read the markets and the different charging rates levied by financial advisors. How to use Morningstar for fund information, Investors.com for what the market is doing and various other references will improve my knowledge and get me more interested in reviewing my investments regularly.

The book has been well researched by the author and follows a logical sequence, making it easy to put down and pick up again or to use as a reference point when looking for investment information. It stresses that portfolios need to be managed on a full time basis, which most private individuals can't do and so they need professional help.

I give the book a 5 star rating and recommend it to all ISACO clients and prospects, anyone who wants to improve the performance of their portfolios and financial advisors."

John Wallace, ISACO Client and Ex-CIO of One of the World's Leading International Banks

"How to Make Money in ISAs and SIPPs by Stephen Sutherland is a book explaining how to do exactly as the title suggests. I agreed to read and review the book as a client of ISACO and I must admit I was not looking forward to it as I always find this sort of book quite boring to read.

I am an avid investor, always have been, but I do find reading about the subject quite dull, which is probably why I have never been any good at it! I actually read this book in just three evenings, I found it very easy to read and I didn't want to put it down. I found the chapter for beginners very informative and easy to understand and this ease of reading carried on throughout the rest of the book. Graphs and illustrations helped to explain things in a very straightforward and unstuffy manner.

I also found the sincerity of the author coming through, at one point apologising for not guiding his clients into a cash park prior to the stock market's plummet in 2008. I would thoroughly recommend this book to investors old, new and those considering becoming clients of ISACO. I award the book full marks, five stars out of five."

Paul Parkin, ISACO Client and Business Owner

"How to Make Money in ISAs and SIPPs is exactly what every modern individual needs to know about investing!

As a successful businessman in my own field of dentistry and having sold two companies in the past eighteen months for 7 figures each, you would think that I would have a firm grasp on the best way to invest my hard earned money. Unfortunately, you would be wrong! When it came to ISAs and SIPPs it literally seemed like a different world, where everyone talked in code and I would often feel more confused after a session with my previous financial advisor than when I had started.

How to Make Money in ISAs and SIPPs has given me a truly detailed insight into this mythical world and has explained everything in a commonsensical way. It details every aspect I could possibly have wanted explaining in layman's terms, it was so concise and simple to understand that everyone from a novice investor to a sophisticated one would read it with ease.

Stephen's way of breaking down the financial world's barriers is refreshing and insightful, and being an avid reader of investment/lifestyle books I feel this is a MUST READ!

The table explaining the investment amounts/returns of a couple who had invested in ISAs from the beginning was a light bulb moment for me, and convinced me that this style of investment was for me. Coupled with the fact that, as a busy individual, I could not put aside the time to research the markets/funds, the ability to have someone knowledgeable, trustworthy and helpful to contact is fantastic!

This book should be on the essential reading list of every adult, whether interested in investing or not. Once they had read the book, they will have the essential tools needed to understand ISAs and SIPPs and will have a new found enthusiasm to apply this knowledge to improve their lives! It takes the power away from the financial advisors and puts it back into the hands of the individual.

My only negative comment on the book would be how each chapter tries to 'hook' you into the next chapter. It almost reads like a series of articles in a monthly magazine. These are not needed. The book is giving you so much easily digested knowledge that you cannot put it down! No one will read a chapter and put it down for a few weeks. Once you start reading you want to read on, and on, and on!

This book gets 5 out of 5 and goes alongside *Rich Dad, Poor Dad* in being one of the only books to instantaneously change the way I view a topic! Well done Stephen for all your hard work!"

Dr Lance Knight BDS
Founder of Ultimate Smile Spa and Instore Dental

"Stephen Sutherland's book *How to Make Money in ISAs and SIPPs* does exactly what it says on the tin. Stephen cuts through the jargon to make investment understandable. With a demanding full-time job,

I don't have time to make detailed market assessments and need a fast-track approach like Stephen's. It works for me. Rating: *****"

Neal McCrea, ISACO Client, IT Sales Professional and Successful ISA/SIPP Investor

"I rate Stephen's book five out of five stars. The first thing to say is what a great improvement it is on Stephen's previous work, *Liquid Millionaire*. Don't get me wrong. *Liquid Millionaire* was full of really good information that seemed to make sense. It was good enough to convince me that Stephen had something and to become an ISACO client, and shadow invest with at least part of my assets. The problem was that it read far too much like an advertisement for ISACO, and originally that almost put me off.

This is an entirely different work. It reads far more as it should, which is to say, it reads like a populist teaching tool (as opposed to an academic one designed for an examination course). The ISACO 'advert', such as it is, is tucked away as an appendix at the end, and is suitably low key. I feel sure that if I had read this work instead of *Liquid Millionaire* a few years ago, I would have had no doubt about following Stephen Sutherland.

There is a great deal of important information and ideas in the work, too much for a detailed analysis. Some of it is quite complicated, and several of the chapters probably need to be read, digested for a couple of days, and then reread, particularly if the reader is new to investing.

But I would like to pick out two parts for particular comment. Firstly, the detailed instructions for using the 'Morningstar' website are very useful. Getting to know the ins and outs of this website is a must for those hoping to pick the best funds for investing, and Stephen's explanation is as good as you are likely to get.

Secondly, the information on investment timing should help to take some of the guesswork out of it. In particular, his examples of the 'cup-with-handle' signal are particularly clear, and since reading this work, I have been able to spot them in historical charts quite easily. Having previously read the works of William J. O'Neil (who Stephen holds in high regard, I believe), with all his historical charts with examples of cup-with-handle signals, I had great difficulty in actually seeing what he was talking about.

So, overall, I approve strongly of Stephen's efforts here. But I need to make one small criticism. For a couple to put more than £20,000 a year into ISAs, they would either need to be earning far above average, or have already accumulated a fair amount of assets. That's OK for the likes of me, retired, mortgage paid off, with a combination of accumulated savings, an occupational pension, plus something inherited from deceased parents.

But for the likes of most people (like my son and daughter), working on average or below average earnings, and with a mortgage, this is all pie in the sky. But the basic message for them is the same. They may not be able to put away enough to retire on a million pounds, but even the one or two hundred put away each month will accumulate over the long term.

I think Stephen should have included examples for people for whom putting anywhere near the maximum into an ISA or SIPP is simply not an option. In fact, if the book has not yet gone to print, I suggest he does this before it goes to print, and if it already has gone to print, I would suggest this as something for a second edition!"

Alan Bridewell, ISACO Client and Retired School Teacher

"This is a well written, user-friendly book. The concepts are explained in plain English so that even people with no financial training such as me, can understand the concepts and philosophy. It is also very interesting to read Stephen's own success story and how he got into this 'business' as a motivation to us all. It is not a get rich quick scheme but what he does outline does appear to work to increase one's wealth given time, diligence and the power of SIPPs and ISAs. 5 stars."

Professor Sanjiv Jari, BSc(Hons), MBChB, FRCS[Eng], FRCS[Tr & Orth], ISACO Client and Consultant Knee, Lower Limb & Orthopaedic Sports Medicine Surgeon. www.thekneedoc.co.uk

How to Make Money in ISAs and SIPPs is a basic to an in-depth understanding of how ISAs and SIPPs can allow the average person to accumulate a tax-free fund, which can be used to provide additional income for retirement or the finer things in life. I personally read Stephen Sutherland's book *Liquid Millionaire* in 2010 and decided to shadow invest with Stephen and Paul and have luckily not looked back since.

Having never thought about share funds before but having a Cash ISA, it was actually the best thing I could have done. Leaving your money to be managed by a fund manager and receiving a statement once a year to tell you how it has performed in all honesty is madness. The books that Stephen has written make it so easy to manage your own funds or if you don't fancy this, simply shadow his every move.

Having now a little more understanding of ISAs and SIPPs, it made very easy but interesting reading.

The key points of interest to me personally were:

1) Hidden charges and fees.
2) How fund supermarkets make it simple, easy and cheap to buy and sell funds.
3) The benefits from investing in funds and spreading the risk.
4) Morningstar is a must, with so much invaluable information at your fingertips.
5) The ability to move your money out of funds and into cash when the market is going south.

Finally, anybody who has money invested in an ISA or SIPP should read this book. It makes easy and excellent reading for the up and coming novice investor. I would rate it 5-star reading."

Barry Young, ISACO Client and Estimating Engineer

"Having read Stephen's earlier book, *Liquid Millionaire* which in itself was a great informative read, I was expecting much of the same with this new book, just minor updates to be honest.

However, I am greatly surprised and pleased by the new information within this book – particularly on Self Invested Personal Pensions or SIPPs. With all the doom and gloom, negative press about the financial markets of late it is a must read as it gives hope to us ourselves to take charge of our own financial future, with the support of real honest, no nonsense people such as Stephen and Paul Sutherland and the whole team at ISACO. I would highly encourage all readers to focus on 'Chapter 4: Charges, Fees, and Fund Supermarkets' – this is a real eye opener!

As most of you probably reading this review, like I, may have a company pension and you have to watch it ride the markets in both directions, making very small gains and worrying future projections based on typical 3% realistic mid level growth. It's disheartening and I certainly felt concerned every year reviewing my pension statement. A huge part of this is due to hidden fees, trail commissions, high fund fees and limited fund choice. My own company pension had a choice of only 12 funds, with fees ranging from 2% to as high as 5.5%!

Another aspect of this poor performance is watching your pension being locked into the market so that if we have a global bad spell such as in 2008 and 2011 so do your investments such as pensions. Having read the book and then armed with the knowledge to ask the questions about my own fees etc I was shocked at how much they were and how much I had lost over the last 14 years due to the compounding effect from the fees. So I decided to take action and contact ISACO directly to learn more, and the rest as they say, is history.

What most people don't know is that a SIPP not only enables you to choose (as you can with your stocks and shares ISAs) from thousands of funds with very low fees, you actually have the choice to move your investment to a 'Cash Park' so if the global economy is bearish or going down as in 2008, your investment is safe in cash and even earning some small interest! As I am no expert in picking the right fund AND a fund with low or no fees, or the actual timing to switch funds, I decided to simply use the premium shadow service of ISACO, who have achieved attractive annual growth (independently confirmed).

It really is a no brainer – the money I unknowingly spent on fees with my company pension more than pays for this service – my SIPP pension pot as well my stocks and shares ISAs have gained considerably since joining the service. If you are worried about paperwork and form filling, don't be – this is all taken care of by ISACO.

Together with the 'Daily Market Updates' and monthly 'Big Picture' I receive by email, the simple fund platform that I use to view my investments on my smart phone and the unlimited support from ISACO, I can honestly say I am not worried about my financial future as I feel I am in control. I am more than happy with my experience with ISACO (I consider Stephen and Paul as my friends) and I am happy to personally discuss this with anyone, such is my belief in them. The book and service is certainly 5 stars."

Abdul Khan, ISACO Client and Electrical Engineer

"This excellent book is a must-read for both those new to investing and those more experienced in the subject. I read it from cover to cover and thoroughly enjoyed confirming what I already knew but also adding so much more to my previous knowledge. The book is well structured and Stephen has a relaxed and easy way of explaining what can be a difficult subject.

I liked the chapters on timing the buys and exits and also managing your portfolio and creating an income for life. Some chapters – like the one on charges and fees – I had to read twice in order to take in all the new information that was presented. There were so many golden nuggets I would definitely give it a 5 star rating.

If you want financial security for you and your family then I recommend this book to you. It might just change your life."

Melvyn Rosenthal, ISACO Client, Retired Dentist and Property Investor

"One of the great maxims of success in any field is 'If you want to be successful in a particular field, find other people who have a track record of success in that field, and follow their methods.' This is the concept that Stephen Sutherland has not only used himself to establish a fifteen-year track record of successful financial investing, but it is also the basis of his book; he invites the reader to follow this success maxim by presenting the methods that have ensured his own financial success.

He does this by laying out, in detail and in sequence, the facets that an investor would need to construct and manage a financial portfolio. This, when coupled with the tax-efficient vehicles of ISAs and SIPPs, give the reader an unparalleled opportunity to take maximum advantage of the generosity of the taxman and the stock market.

The book is basically in two halves: the first half aimed at the relative newcomer to investing, who is given a thorough grounding in basic concepts. The second half is aimed at those who have mastered the fundamentals and are ready to reap the rewards of following a disciplined approach to investing.

Yes, the book requires assiduous reading (probably several times) and attention to detail, but the end result will be well worth the effort. I only wish this book had been written twenty years ago! I will certainly be buying copies for my (adult) children. Star Rating: ***** ”

David Parsons, ISACO Client and Private Investor

"Having been a client and 'shadow investor' of Stephen Sutherland's company, I can state that to the best of my knowledge, the principles outlined in this book are those he adheres to in his daily market analysis. Anyone who is in the fortunate situation of being able to start investing in a SIPP and/or ISAs *before* they retire could not find better advice than this book offers.

Unfortunately, I chanced upon his *Liquid Millionaire* book late in life, but having 'shadowed' his personal investments, am pleased to see constant double-digit figures in my ISAs annual percentage profit column.

This latest book is, in most part, easy to follow and understand, is well illustrated with screenshots etc, and assuming you had the 10,000 hours to commit to studying the subject (as recommended for learning most new skills) would result in the required outcome of financial benefits. Failing that, you could do a lot worse than taking up the author's offer to 'shadow' him.

Hoping that the book achieves the success it deserves, and that the royalties donated to Christies accrue accordingly. I give this book a 5* rating."

Jim Law, ISACO Client and Private Investor

"I enjoyed the book immensely and found it a mine of important information which will be invaluable to self investors whatever their experience.

I have recently retired and if the information contained in the book had been available to me some 30 odd years ago I'm sure that my ISA and SIPP would be larger in value than at present, having for many years relied on the usual savings schemes offered by banks and societies.

As mentioned in the book there are a lot of questions that should be asked of IFA's and other establishments offerings products before choices are made. The uninformed I believe, trust the industry too much to their detriment. There is a lot of information which Stephen uncovers that most of us would never have known about, which is of great importance when adding up the costs of saving.

I first heard of Stephen on the internet and read his first book *Liquid Millionaire*. I became a client of ISACO shortly after and have no regrets. This book is written in no nonsense, plain English which is refreshing, easy to read and understand. Stephen is certainly passionate about his favourite subject and being self taught has left no stone unturned. You find yourself caught up in his enthusiasm.

This book also contains all the information you need to educate yourself and make the correct decisions for your saving plans present and future. In my honest opinion it is the reference bible for the self investor and I highly recommend it to you all. Top score on a scale of 1 to 5 a definite 5 star. Buy it, you won't regret your decision."

Andy Jackson, ISACO Client and Private Investor

"Rather refreshingly there is no need to describe what the book is about as it is exactly as the title suggests; a straight talking title from a straight talking author. That said I thought I would any way. The book gives an excellent overview of the benefits of ISAs and SIPPs (I learnt some new things about SIPPs) and a good way to limit the charges you pay. It also shares with you different types of investment funds, how to pick them and when to buy and sell.

The only chapter that gets a bit technical is the one on gauging stock market direction; if you like charts you will like that chapter. There is also a chapter on behavioural psychology which will almost certainly resonate with everyone who reads it; it certainly did with me. Stephen explains how to manage your portfolio and gives some very useful tips on what tools you can use to help you do this. The books rounds off with details of Stephen's 5 Step Plan for creating an income for life and why he thinks the next 10 years could be a 'Golden Opportunity'.

The chapters I personally found most interesting were the one on SIPPs and the one on behavioural finance. Until reading this book I was mistakenly under the impression that SIPPs were as inflexible as a normal pension scheme and cost a small fortune to run; not so it seems, so something I will certainly be looking into over the coming months. I found the chapter about the psychology traits that play such an important part in one's investment decisions fascinating. I found myself thinking 'so that is why I did not sell when I should have' and 'so that is why I did not get back in when I should have'. I may still make the same mistakes but at least now I know what causes them so I will hopefully make the right choices going forward. I would highly recommend this book to anyone thinking of investing in equities, whether that is inside a tax efficient ISA, JISA or SIPP wrapper or outside of them.

That said, there are plenty of 'nuggets' of information for new and experienced investors alike. For those of you who think books on stock market investment are all too often technically complicated (I do) this book will be a pleasant surprise, definitely worth 4 stars. The reason I did not give it 5 stars is that some of it was what I had read in Stephen's previous book and I also did not have the 'cannot put it down' feeling with it."

Steven Ball, ISACO Client, HR Manager and Property Investor

"In this book by Stephen Sutherland he sets out in a very logical and thorough way to share his views and experiences on the power of informed investing in ISAs and SIPPs in order to maximise their taxation benefits for individual investors.

Stephen shares his experiences over the last 13 years in an open, honest and very transparent way, all of which is done in a very informal manner, yet hitting all the right notes when it comes to facts and figures. In the 13 years since Stephen started out on his investment strategy he readily acknowledges that he has made mistakes, which he quickly recognised and learned from in order to avoid again in the future.

His comments clearly show how well he has researched the market and he is not afraid of helping readers avoid the pitfalls and gain benefit from the extensive investment knowledge he has gained – something which he admits is mainly 'self taught'. Stephen hides nothing from the reader and openly shares his knowledge – I particularly like 'Chapter 6 – How to Pick a Good Fund' – this for me, is the most powerful chapter in the book and if you only read this then you can be excused for not reading the rest.

As a relatively new client of ISACO, this book was an enlightening read and helped me understand more about investing, even though I have been an active investor for over 25 years. I would strongly recommend you read Stephen's book from cover to cover and don't be afraid to learn from it and put into practice what you learn. This book will appeal to investors of all types – a must for those just venturing into the world of investing and equally for those who believe they are seasoned investors – my view is that you are never too experienced to stop learning – and any investor at any stage in between. My star rating is 5 – excellent."

Don Butterworth, ISACO Client and Private Investor

"Stephen has written the bible for ISA/SIPP investors – a truly comprehensive guide for those wishing to take control of their financial security. The book is easy to read and contains a wealth of knowledge and expert guidance on all aspects of investment success. There are gems of little understood areas, such as the impact of charges on ISA/SIPP performance. This is the sort of stuff that a conventional IFA won't reveal to you. The book is essential bedtime reading for anyone aiming to maximize returns in their pension."

Dominic Bannister, ISACO Client and Physiotherapist

"An excellent 5 star book that offers a very straightforward explanation about self-directed ISA and SIPP investment. It avoids unnecessary financial jargon or complexity, yet provides a structure and method which support a logical approach to personal investment decisions. In particular, the guidance and illustrations about fund selection, basic interpretation of charts and market timing, are all very welcome and serve to unravel what can otherwise become an overwhelming challenge. It is a great addition which will get regular use for both quick reference and further development."

Paul Kirby, ISACO Client and Private Investor

"Stephen's latest book provides the tools and techniques that, when used with discipline and combined with modest capital, can ensure you accumulate vast amounts of wealth over time. I only wish he had written and I had acted upon it years ago. Essential '5 star' reading like *Rich Dad Poor Dad* – for those focused individuals with years on their side and a desire to rise above the crowd."

Richard Hetherington, ISACO Client and Business Consultant

"I really liked the fact that this is an easy read that outlines in simple language everything you need to know about pensions and ISAs. Each subject is covered in detail that will leave any reader more confident about taking hold of their own financial destiny. The bit that works for me is that it looks at targets that are achievable. 5 stars."

Martin Lloyd, ISACO Client and Private Investor

"I greatly enjoyed it. This 5 star book flows well and gives a very succinct account of how to invest properly. I will be both buying copies for clients and recommending it when it is available for general release."

Iain Cahill, ISACO Client and Founder of Art of Wealth

"A fabulous and insightful 5 star read. I particularly liked the chapters on picking a good fund and when to buy and when to exit, where there are so many really useful pieces of information that have been written in such a way that the average private investor can understand. Stephen Sutherland has made serious money in ISAs and SIPPs and he shares his knowledge quite openly and shows you how he actually manages his portfolio by sharing with you all the tools he uses on a day-to-day basis. The chapter on fund charges and fees was a real eye-opener for me."

Pete Davidson, ISACO Client and Estate Manager

"Dear Stephen, Wow… I really loved reading your latest book! I thoroughly enjoyed reading it – from cover to cover – every word stated in it is absolutely priceless, and has the potential to make the reader very rich indeed. The knowledge you have gained through your own hard work and determination is crammed into every page, and as the reader, I felt like I was being taught by the Jedi Master! It really was wonderful to read and I can't thank you enough for allowing me to review it.

Comments on the content

1) It is very well written, in an easy-to-read format, friendly language and very easy to understand.
2) Lovely concise and easy to absorb titles and sub-headings – good for referring to at a later date once the book is read. I will be reading it many times as the information it contains is solid gold.
3) Packed with educational information on fees and charges that I found to be eye-opening and very educational. I wish I had read this earlier in my investing career.
4) 'When to buy' and 'when to sell' information is potentially worth millions of pounds.
5) Wonderful advice on adopting a long-term view to investing,

coping with drops in your portfolio, advice on funding your retirement . . . outstanding information that is life-changing for the reader.

The only slight criticism I may have is that some parts of the book are in your first book *Liquid Millionaire*.

Out of ten I am tempted to give it eleven!! ;)

Thanks so much for writing this book Stephen, I will do my very best to learn every single fact in it . . . and one day I may be Skywalker to your Yoda ;)"

Simon Webb, ISACO Client and Bridge Engineer

"This is an excellent book that is written in clear and concise terms that would be helpful to anyone who has an interest in investing for their future. The information contained therein summarises thousands of hours work by the author and I can confirm that I have used his methodology to source funds for my own investments.

This book would be suitable for a novice as well as a more experienced investor and offers an insight into the workings of the stock market and the way fund managers influence prices. For me personally, I have found this book very helpful and would have no hesitation in giving it a five star rating."

Alan Johnson, ISACO Client and Sales Director

"How to Make Money in ISAs and SIPPs is a fantastic book that's easy to read, easy to understand and it's broken down into easy to digest chapters. I thoroughly enjoyed reading this book. I found it

so easy to digest and understand the charts, unlike lots of other so-called experts who make it very complicated to follow.

This book contains very good advice on how to invest and it's all explained in very simple language. Everyone who wants to save for their own and their family's future should own and read a copy (I am sure we are all guilty of owning books that we will eventually get round to reading or finishing). On a separate note, I'm one of Stephen's clients and through 'shadowing' him I have seen a healthy improvement in my investments over the last 3 years."

Tony Diamond, ISACO Client and Private Investor

"How to Make Money in ISAs and SIPPs is an essential, enjoyable and stimulating read for all personal investors looking to create wealth in a way that is straightforward and easy to follow.

The author writes with a clarity that is open, transparent and honest in its approach; and overall provides an invaluable lesson in understanding Trend Investing and why it is so important and financially rewarding to follow investment principles, not the herd!"

Neil Sutherland, ISACO Client and Independent Financial Adviser and Director of Sutherland IFA Limited

"Stephen Sutherland takes the lid off fund investment – offering an insightful appraisal of the opportunities ahead, and how to develop a winning formula. If you seriously want to protect and grow your wealth in a tax-efficient way then this book is essential reading! It's very well structured, and contains some really practical information – I will give it 5 stars!"

Roger Allison, ISACO Client and Sales Executive

"I am not a financial expert and have been using Stephen's shadow investment service for a few years. Having read this book, I am now even more confident that I am following the correct strategy. Stephen's book is easy to read and he uses simple terms to clearly explain concepts that could be overwhelming.

The book follows a logical sequence and I discovered that he answered my questions as I was asking them. I now understand what Stephen bases his investment decisions on, and I also understand where I went wrong in the past and why. Stephen is clearly passionate about his subject, but at the same time grounded enough to give me the confidence that shadowing his decisions will help me achieve my long-term financial objectives."

Elsabe Smit, ISACO Client and Seasoned Motivation
and Development Professional www.elsabesmit.com

"Right from the start this book delivers straight forward, easy to follow advice for increasing your wealth through ISA and SIPP investments. Written in plain English, Stephen shares vital knowledge for beginners as well as experienced investors and touches on the psychology of market behaviour, an area of investment often ignored by beginners. I particularly enjoyed the step by step guide on how to go about being a DIY investor, showing how to find the right funds for your portfolio, risk assessment, when to buy and when to sell.

All in all an invaluable guide to investment success without paying tax which I can't wait to implement with some hard earned savings."

Clive Andrews, ISACO Client and Service Manager

"I read *How to Make Money in ISAs and SIPPs* from cover to cover and I thought it absolutely excellent, certainly worth 5 stars. In my view, anyone managing their own ISAs and SIPPs should have a copy to hand. Even experienced investors, not only those investing in ISAs and SIPPs, would do well to have a copy, as I'm sure they will find in it many useful nuggets of information, either new to them or ones they had forgotten about. Stephen must have put an enormous amount of time and effort into it and the result is a really valuable addition to my investment library, as I am sure it will be for many others."

John Clark, ISACO Client and Business Owner

"The book is absolutely top class and the key things for me are as follows:

1. The Performance Quadrant and its understanding of what you can control and what you cannot.
2. The impact of charges, both present and future, upon the profitability of the investment.
3. Identifying fund managers who have outperformed in both the long and short terms.
4. That investing conservatively is high risk not low risk in the long term.
5. The depth of knowledge that Morningstar requires to understand the fund choices available and the conclusion that I should let ISACO do the work instead."

Derek Shears, ISACO Client and Private Investor

"UK investors read this book! *How to Make Money in ISAs and*

SIPPs by Stephen Sutherland should be required reading for any new investor in the UK.

It contains a mix of investment philosophy, principles and practical advice that you simply won't get in most other books. Most importantly it comes from a man who 'practices what he preaches.' He shares his journey with us, including the mistakes he has made and the lessons he has learned. This is invaluable as the investor's walk is a difficult one, but Stephen removes the rose tinted glasses from the reader, whilst leaving us with a sense of hope for the future and just as importantly, giving clear investment strategies.

His approach of using ISAs and SIPPs is invaluable, potentially saving the reader who applies these strategies thousands of pounds. I particularly enjoyed Chapter 9 on investor behaviour, seeing my past self in the descriptions of how we can act irrationally when investing. Chapter 7 on fund timing would be a real revelation to most new investors, guarding against rookie mistakes that derail us before we even get going.

I thoroughly recommend this book to anyone in the UK looking for practical, well rounded investment advice."

Andrew Tait, ISACO Client and Business Owner

"This is an excellent book. You wouldn't think a book about investing could be a good read but this actually is! Stephen has an easy style of writing that makes understanding potentially complex issues easy.

He covers difficult subjects like which funds to choose and

importantly, when to buy and sell, in a way that is uncomplicated. If you have wondered how a logically minded person should invest then you must read this book – I thoroughly recommend it and give it five stars!"

Colin Bennett, ISACO Client and Safety Consultant

"I give *How to Make Money in ISAs and SIPPs* five stars! It is a great addition to Stephen's previous book, *Liquid Millionaire*. I like Stephen's simple yet detailed approach to selecting funds through an ISA and SIPP, the book is a must read if you are looking to gain smarter returns.

Stephen's strategy and the (HIRE CAR) formula that ISACO use will help you build a quality, balanced investment portfolio for life! Not many people are aware of such advantages when investing through ISAs and SIPPs, yet this book helps separate the wheat from the chaff.

Shadowing 800 lb gorilla investors is something I've always wanted to learn more about and Stephen explains exactly how you can follow their lead. I personally was not aware of the wide investment streams SIPPs have to offer, and also the fact that SIPPs allow you to gain a tax-free lump sum when you retire.

The Performance Quadrant explained in the book was amazing! The material within this book is easy to understand and Stephen will take you through it step by step. If you're looking to build tax-free wealth then this book is for you."

Matthew Dorrington, ISACO Client and Private Investor

"*How to Make Money in ISAs and SIPPs* is an extensive tableau of the ISA and SIPP investment world. Of course as an ISACO 'shadow' investor, it's all pretty easy for me in practice, in that I just do what Stephen does and try to maximise my annual ISA and SIPP contributions – easy really! This book is a welcome and timely refresh of Stephen's comprehensive guide to the workings, tactics and potential pitfalls for investors who are active in the ISA and SIPP market.

The book is well structured in a thoughtful and logical way, with the workings of the various market functions and dynamics explained in clear terms that are easily absorbed by a non-professional, as jargon is avoided or unpicked. *How to Make Money in ISAs and SIPPs* highlights the impact that fund charges can have on portfolio returns over an extended period, which I found was particularly valuable, and something that is now very much on my radar as I consider the investment options and market player offerings available.

Credible and relevant personal insights woven throughout the book ensure that it has a relaxed narrative feel, avoiding any feeling of dry, academic text book material. I'm happy to give it a 5 star rating in terms of delivering the intended business outcome – an easy to access, compete guide to helping individuals taking control of their financial futures by systematically exploiting the growth and income potential offered by investing in ISAs and SIPPs."

Simon Rollason, ISACO Client and Management Consultant

"I read Stephen Sutherland's previous book, *Liquid Millionaire* about 4 years ago and found it excellent. This book is an updated version of *Liquid Millionaire*, suitable for up to 2014.

I have found this book useful as a refresher to re-learn about ISAs and SIPPs. On a personal note I can find these subjects very tedious, not coming from a financial background but Stephen Sutherland explains the subject in a way is very easy to understand and makes the subjects very interesting.

I would recommend this book as a reference to anyone who wants to find out how ISAs work and anyone who wants to manage their own SIPP. This book would be my first point of reference.

If I do have any criticisms about the book, the only thing I would find useful would be to have an appendix for all the abbreviations at the back of the book, which I can refer to whilst reading the book. Well recommended."

Simon Berman, ISACO Client and Biomedical Scientist

"I bought Stephen's first book *Liquid Millionaire* in early 2010. By the summer, I was a client I loved it so much. This book pretty much follows on and expands on the ideas in the first book.

I particularly liked the section on fees and charges, as this is a complex, difficult to understand area, and it is explained in a clear and concise way for the non-financial person. Stephen shows how much of our own money is being quietly eaten up by them and how the financial industry is changing to become more transparent.

I would recommend buying both books and reading them together. I used to invest in ISAs each year just from newspaper tips on best funds. I had no strategy, I didn't know what, or when to buy or sell. This book will give you a strategy and many tips on other places to find financial help. I'm so glad I discovered ISACO and Stephen's books. They have changed my financial life!"

Ian C. Oakley, ISACO Client and Locum Community Pharmacist

"Another motivational and educational read from Stephen Sutherland. He has used the information included in his previous book *Liquid Millionaire* but expanded on this greatly.

Even experienced investors should read the whole book. I want to pick out two chapters that I found very enlightening. 'Chapter 4: Charges, Fees and Fund Supermarkets' is an eye opener and has information all investors should be aware of (don't assume financial institutions are on your side!). I also found 'Chapter 10: How to Manage Your Portfolio' to be very useful and worth reading over. The stress is on actively managing your portfolio.

Even though I have read *Liquid Millionaire* more than once, the new book includes Stephen's latest research and ideas and has expanded my knowledge about successful investment strategy. Every investor should read this book."

Ian Dyson, ISACO Client and IT Analyst

"This is a book that is invaluable and should be available in senior schools from the Ministry of Education. It should certainly be read by teachers of sixth form pupils and recommended beyond for those entering the world of employment.

To quote Richard Koch: 'Few people take objectives really seriously . . . those who achieve the most are selective as well as determined'.

The full understanding of money and appreciation of the best way to put it to work for us to provide a better life that we all seek can be found in this book.

It states that SIPPs and ISAs are 'two of the UK's best kept secrets' – but actually they aren't secrets at all. Despite being available for years the majority of people, including myself, have criminally failed to recognise the opportunity they provide and it shows we have been too complacent.

The majority of investors have always followed the well worn path of seeking the advice of professional advisors but in recent years we have been shown that many professionals fail to beat market indices. Furthermore, we have learned that much of our investments are swallowed up by fees that have left our pensions bereft of expected profits.

Now all that can be changed by this book. Tax-efficient investing is for everybody – with no exceptions – and this book will show you the 'What, How and When' in the simplest of terms without any jargon. Put simply, it is a must-read for anyone who desires to improve their own financial lot in this life.

Had I read and acted on this book as a young man it would have made my life very much richer and more fulfilling today. I urge you to read this book and, most important of all, act on its advice."

Tim Spring, ISACO Client and Private Investor

"For me as an investor using ISACO's shadow investment strategy, this book is the A-Z of how Stephen selects the best funds to invest in. He outlines his financial goals and explains in detail how best to achieve them; the book considers the most efficient way to invest in the market; using ISA and SIPP wrappers, and minimising fees.

Stephen also explains timing is key, when to buy, when to switch or when to sit it out on the side lines in cash; all critical decisions to help you hold on to your gains. Market direction and getting in sync with the big players are two major market indicators that Stephen reviews every day, using analytical data to make investment decisions. The best part of this book for me is it's a simple read that explains a complex financial environment. I would recommend this book to anyone thinking about investing over the long term to secure their financial future."

John Forrest, ISACO Client and Operations Manager

Notes

1 www.amazon.co.uk/Financial-Times-Selecting-Shares-Perform/dp/0273712675/ref=pd_sim_b_5

2 www.richardkoch.net/category/blog

3 HM Revenue & Customs: Individual Savings Accounts (ISA) Statistics.

http://www.hmrc.gov.uk/statistics/isas/statistics.pdf

4 HM Revenue & Customs: Individual Savings Accounts (ISA) Statistics.

http://www.hmrc.gov.uk/statistics/isas/statistics.pdf

5 HM Revenue & Customs: Personal Pension Statistics.

http://www.hmrc.gov.uk/statistics/pension-stats/pensions-intro.pdf

6 HM Revenue & Customs: Personal Pension Statistics.

http://www.hmrc.gov.uk/statistics/pension-stats/pensions-intro.pdf

7 FT adviser.

http://www.ftadviser.com/2012/11/23/pensions/sipps/income-drawdown-for-sipps-making-the-right-choice-8uUCKcan4IeezTx1FKtxyI/article.html

8 Dalbar.

http://moneyover55.about.com/od/howtoinvest/a/average investor.htm

9 Morningstar – 'The study of the decade'. http://trendfollowing.com/whitepaper/The%20Study%20of%20the%20Decade.pdf

10 In a 2010 poll conducted by Allianz Life Insurance Co of North America on people aged 44 to 75, more than three in five (61%) said they feared depleting their assets more than they feared dying.

11 *24 Essential Lessons for Investment Success* – William J. O'Neil.

12 December 31st 2008 – December 31st 2013. Annual returns: Stephen Sutherland 14.5%, FTSE 100 8.8%. Investment performance verified by Independent Executives Ltd.

13 Reading taken December 24th 2012.

14 Reading taken December 24th 2012.

15 IFS Level 3 Certificate for Financial Advisers.

16 Yahoo! Finance: Cumulative return (December 31st 1997 – December 31st

2013) Stephen Sutherland 91.3%, FTSE 100 31.1%. Investment performance verified by Independent Executives Ltd.

17   Stephen Sutherland ISA account returns verified by Independent Executives Ltd.

18   15th November 2012: Internal estimation of total ISA and pension assets owned by ISACO Investment Team and ISACO premium clients.

19   FT.com.

http://www.ft.com/cms/s/2/836a4c76-d309-11df-9ae9-00144feabdc0.html#axzz2cUuPhGDH

20   FT.com.

http://www.ft.com/cms/s/2/836a4c76-d309-11df-9ae9-00144feabdc0.html#axzz2cUuPhGDH

21   Department for Work and Pensions, April 2010.

22   Association of British Insurers and James Charles, *The Times*, January 2008.

23   FT Adviser.

http://www.ftadviser.com/2012/02/13/funds-and-data/investors-don-t-realise-what-they-re-being-charged-OjugcU7hgXHJpM88rzRpfL/article.html

24   FT.com.

http://www.ft.com/cms/s/0/8a898374-ac09-11e2-9e7f00144feabdc0.html#axzz2Rmdy3dK8

25   FT.com, July 10th 2011 – 'Backlash over fund performance fees'.

26   This is MONEY.co.uk, January 31st 2012 "New fight against 'dishonest' fund fees pushes new way to make ISAs cheaper".

http://www.thisismoney.co.uk/money/investing/article-2094376/New-fight-dishonest-fund-fees-aims-make-ISAs-cheaper—trueandfaircampaign-com.html

27   Standard Life Investments.

http://uk.standardlifeinvestments.com/U_KIID_GB_UHQO_Inst_Acc_Acc_GBP_EN/getLatest.pdf

28   MoneyWeek.   http://moneyweek.com/we-like-investment-trusts-but-they-need-to-cut-their-fees-60900/

29   Which.co.uk – active versus passive investment.

30   Trustnet.

http://www.trustnet.com/News/381589/cheap-tracker-funds-thrash-expensive-rivals/

31   FT.com.

http://www.ft.com/cms/s/2/7e36a024-c87a-11dd-b86f-000077b07658.html#axzz2JoPR7atU

32   Yahoo! Finance: Cumulative return (December 31st 1997 – December 31st 2013) Stephen Sutherland 91.3%, FTSE 100 31.1%.

33   Yahoo! Finance: Period taken January 1st 1975 to December 31st 1999.

34   *How to Make Money in Stocks* – William J. O'Neil Third edition – Page 49.

35   Reading taken Saturday January 12th 2013.

36   Investors.com.

http://education.investors.com/faq.aspx?nav=secondIBDUAsk

37   Markowitz, 1952.

38   Sharpe, 1964.

39   Kahneman and Riepe, 1998.

40   Swanlowpark.

http://www.swanlowpark.co.uk/ftseannual.jsp

41   Yahoo! Finance: Cumulative return (December 31st 1997 – December 31st 2013) Stephen Sutherland 91.3% FTSE 100 31.1%. Investment performance verified by Independent Executives Ltd.

42   Annual returns over 5 year period: Stephen Sutherland 14.5%, FTSE 100's 8.8% (December 31st 2008 – December 31st 2013. Investment performance verified by Independent Executives Ltd.

43   Allianz Global Investors – According to calculations by Allianz Economic Research based on the 12th population projection of the Federal Statistical Office of Germany.

44   November 15th 2012: Internal estimation of total ISA and pension assets owned by ISACO Investment Team and ISACO premium clients.

45   Long-term performance: December 31st 1997 – December 31st 2013 Stephen Sutherland 91.3%, FTSE 100 31.1%. 5 year performance: December 31st 2008 – December 31st 2013. ISACO investment performance verified by Independent Executives Ltd.

46   Elroy Dimson, Paul Marsh, and Mike Staunton, Credit Suisse Global Investment Returns Sourcebook 2012.

47   Morningstar – 'The study of the decade'.

http://trendfollowing.com/whitepaper/The%20Study%20of%20the%20Decade.pdf

Index

Page references to charts and screenshots will be in italics. References to Notes will have the letter 'n' following the page number.